A God of Vengeance?

A God of Vengeance?

Understanding the Psalms of Divine Wrath

Erich Zenger

translated by

Linda M. Maloney

Westminster John Knox Press
Louisville, Kentucky

Translated from *Ein Gott der Rache: Feindpsalmen Verstehen,* © Verlag Herder, Freiburg im Breisgau, 1994

English translation © 1996 Westminster John Knox Press

Book design by Jennifer K. Cox
Cover design by Alec Bartsch
Images copyright © 1995 PhotoDisc, Inc.

First edition

Published by Westminster John Knox Press
Louisville, Kentucky

This book is printed on acid-free paper that meets the American National Standards Institute Z39.48 standard. ♾

PRINTED IN THE UNITED STATES OF AMERICA

96 97 98 99 00 01 02 03 04 05 — 10 9 8 7 6 5 4 3 2 1

Library of Congress Cataloging-in-Publication Data

Zenger, Erich, 1939–
    [Gott der Rache?   English]
    A God of vengeance? : understanding the Psalms of divine wrath /
Erich Zenger : translated by Linda M. Maloney. — 1st ed.
      p.   cm.
    Includes bibliographical references (p.   ).
    ISBN 0-664-25637-6 (alk. paper)
    1. Bible. O.T. Psalms—Criticism, interpretation, etc.
2. Anger—Religious aspects—Christianity.   3. Revenge. I. Title.
BS1430.2.Z4613   1996
223'.206—dc20   95-4639

Contents

Preface

The biblical psalms confront us with a world full of enmity and violence. Those who prayed them screamed out their terror before the multiple visages of their enemies, and especially before their God. Indeed, they accuse their own God as an enemy who terrorizes and oppresses them. In the psalms, they struggle against their fears and against the pictures of their enemies that arise out of those fears. The thesis of this book is that the "psalms of enmity" are a way of robbing the aggressive images of the enemies of their destructiveness, and transforming them into constructive forces. Its intention is to bring into focus a unique feature of the biblical book of Psalms that generally goes unrecognized in Christianity, or is simply rejected.

Recent investigations of the topic of violence have repeatedly made clear that the question of "enemy images" is a central one for anthropology and social analysis. The psychoanalyst Thea Bauriedl writes, for example, in her book, *Wege aus der Gewalt: Analyse von Beziehungen* (Freiburg, 2nd ed., 1993):

> For some years now, there has been a good deal of talk about images of the enemy in the German-speaking world, as well as about the danger of those images as precursors of military action and violent confrontations; there has also been discussion of the necessity of eliminating them. But what are enemy images, really? Why do we need them? How do they come into existence, for individuals and groups? Is there a psychic, even a collective-psychic predisposition leading to the development of enemy images? And how does such a disposition come about? How can it be changed? All these are questions of political psychology, or political psychoanalysis. The answers offered by political psychoanalysis can lead us beyond a

mere *appeal* to abolish images of the enemy, because they aid us toward an *understanding* of the mechanisms that are at work in *everyone*. If we can begin to understand that images of the enemy repeatedly arise in ourselves and other people *out of necessity*, as soon as our anxiety in interpersonal conflicts becomes too strong, we will feel less need to depreciate or attack other people when they react, in situations of fear (perhaps even when it is suppressed), with demonization or fantasies of enmity. This means that we will not need to build up enemy images to counter enemy images. We can more easily find ways to help ourselves and others out of this unhappy situation, instead of prolonging the misery through continued devaluations and acts of hostility. . . .

The destruction of images of the enemy is not merely a matter of revising our prejudices or clarifying misunderstandings. The concept of the enemy image really describes a specific *form of relationship* between the one who has developed the image and his or her "enemy." Of course, in some circumstances this "enemy" may really be dangerous, because in such relationships one is often in very genuine danger. If the image of the enemy is understood as the expression of a particular relationship, the dissolution of enemy images also becomes, not the clarification of a *misunderstanding, but the changing of a structure of relationships.* (Pp. 19, 28–29)

The psalms articulate violence, whether experienced or feared, as a relational phenomenon. As poetic prayers, they are the media of linguistic fettering of violence and they open routes away from violence—in light of a God who, as the "God of vengeance," reveals God-defying and life-destroying violence *for what it is,* and keeps alive the vision of a life free from violence. Of course, it is true that the biblical psalms speak of and to this God in a disturbing and often shocking way. In particular, the "psalms of cursing," a label that invites misunderstanding—because they do not curse; they present passionate lament, petition, and desires before God—are a puzzle and a stumbling block for many Christians. For this reason, the postconciliar liturgical reform has even rejected certain psalms as unsuitable for the Catholic church's Liturgy of the Hours, and in an act of magisterial barbarism, it destroyed the poetic form of some psalms by simply eliminating individual verses. I will indicate in this book that this censorship is unnecessary and unacceptable, and will show why that is so. In particular, I will show how the psalms of enmity can help us, so that, in the world of violence in which we must live, we will not despair or be broken.

This book could not have come about, were it not for the reliable assistance of my colleagues in the Departments of the History of Religions and General History of the Old/First Testament at the University of Münster. Thus I am grateful to Ulrike Homberg, Benedikt Jürgens, Resi Koslowski,

Ilse Müllner, Johannes Rienäcker, and Bettina Wagner for their collaboration in the preparation of the manuscript for the press, and for critical questions that have inspired me to refine my ideas and expressions.

ERICH ZENGER

Abbreviations

ATD	Das Alte Testament Deutsch
BBB	Bonner biblische Beiträge
BiKi	*Bibel und Kirche*
BZAW	Beihefte zur *Zeitschrift für die alttestamentliche Wissenschaft*
cf.	confer
dtv	*deutscher Taschenbuchverlag*
EvTh	*Evangelische Theologie*
GHKAT	Hermann Gunkel, Handkommentar zum Alten Testament
HAT	Handbuch zum Alten Testament
JBTh	*Jahrbuch für biblische Theologie*
JNWSL	*Journal of Northwest Semitic Languages*
JSOT	*Journal for the Study of the Old Testament*
MThZ	*Münchener theologische Zeitschrift*
NEB.NT	Neue Echter Bibel, Neue Testament
n.s.	new series
NRSV	New Revised Standard Version
OT	Old Testament
QD	Quaestiones Disputatae
SBM	Stuttgarter biblische Monographien

1

A Complex Problem

Unpleasant and Repulsive Psalms

The psalms of the First Testament need not fear comparison with other poetic works of world literature. The power of their language and imagery has opened the hearts and lips of human beings throughout the centuries: in accusation and praise of God, in pleading and thanksgiving, in doubt and understanding. The biblical psalms have inspired poets and musicians. Antonin Dvorak's *Biblical Songs* and the *Symphony of Psalms* of Igor Stravinsky, the psalm motets of Heinrich Schütz and the psalm compositions of Ludwig van Beethoven grew out of the ancient power of the biblical psalms. Even people who have not been "spoiled" by ecclesial socialization experience, in contact with the psalms, what Ludwig Strauss expressed in this way: "Biblical poetry is a living space into which you can enter, as you might pass into the shade of a primeval olive tree that speaks with the winds of heaven."[1] Even in our own century, poets have frequently written "psalms." These modern psalms do not intend to be religious lyrics, and certainly they are not pious imitations (except for those of "Christian imitators"!). When poets like Bertolt Brecht (cf. his "Augsburger Gedichte") and Paul Celan (cf. his "Psalm" in the volume of poetry titled *Die Niemandsrose*), Ingeborg Bachmann (cf. the poems "Anrufung des großen Bären" or "Psalm"), and Ernesto Cardenal (cf. his "Latin American Psalms") adopt formal elements and metaphors from the biblical psalms in order to create a new language for their social, cultural, and religious criticism in the face of the collapse of traditional conventions of language, but also to articulate authentic visions, their practice documents the utterly inexhaustible poetic potential that lives within the psalms.

It is primarily with and in the psalms that Israel, the people of God, has preserved its identity and its continued vitality, despite all attempts (including those of Christians) to exterminate it. The psalms have assumed a unique place in the history of Christian theology and devotion as well. Of the books of the First Testament most frequently quoted or alluded to in the Christian scriptures, psalms rival the book of Isaiah for first place. They quickly assumed a place of honor in monastic prayer, and then in the personal devotion of all Christians. The psalms, and the "psalm songs" inspired by them, became the programmatic and aggressive poetic texts of the great Reformers and their reforming churches. Psalm verses were taken as life mottos at confirmation, and a verse from a psalm is frequently found at the head of a death notice. In the discussions surrounding the reform of the Catholic church's Liturgy of the Hours, as proposed by the Second Vatican Council, one consensus quickly emerged: the psalms must remain the substance of the divine office.

Of course, it is true that, despite all their fascination and all the approval given to the psalms in general and certain psalms in particular, the objections raised against individual psalms (and, as a consequence, against the whole psalter) have never been silenced. These objections were raised clearly and unmistakably, not only in the discussions before and after the Council: It has become almost a ritual part of pastoral reflections and recommendations intended to introduce people to the practice of praying the psalms to point out, regretfully and with apologies, that the book of Psalms—as lovely as it is—unfortunately has a number of blemishes that one may either overlook in a spirit of Christian generosity or criticize from a Christian point of view. I myself have experienced this, with what almost seems the regularity of natural laws, in giving lectures on the psalms: My theological sympathy is quickly—for the most part, immediately—confronted by the question of the so-called psalms of cursing and vengeance, or with direct quotations from the psalms: "Do you really think that, *as Christians* (the question is never *as Jews* or *as human beings,* and certainly not *as victims of rape*) we can pray this way?"

Will not resistance, lack of understanding, and rejection necessarily find expression when people are asked to recite and meditate, as the "word of God" or as prayers recommended by the authority of the church, the things that are found in the psalm verses about to be quoted? It is true that the intensity of resistance will depend, in individual cases, *partly* on the translation chosen. As illustration, I will quote four translations, in the following sequence: (1) New Revised Standard Version,* (2) Luther's translation (original version), (3) Revised Luther version of 1984 (when it differs from the original Luther translation), and (4) Martin Buber's translation. The sequence also, as a rule, signals an increased sensibility of language. However, the fundamental problem here is not one of translation, but of the offensiveness of the text itself.

I have chosen *seven examples* (which could easily be multiplied) in order to illustrate the problem. Its complexity, of course, must be further examined below.

Example One: Psalm 5:5–7

(NRSV 5:4–6)

For you are not a God who delights in wickedness;
    evil will not sojourn with you.
The boastful will not stand before your eyes;
    you hate all evildoers.
You destroy those who speak lies;
    the LORD abhors the bloodthirsty and deceitful.

(Luther version: Revised and Unrevised)

For you are not a God who is pleased with godless beings;
    the one who is evil does not remain before you.
The boastful do not stand before your eyes;
    you are at enmity with all who do evil.
You kill the liar;
    the LORD is disgusted with the bloodthirsty and the false.

(Martin Buber)

For you are not a deity who desires wickedness,
the one who is wicked cannot be a guest in your house,
Boasters do not present themselves before your eyes,
You hate all who do outrageous things,
those who speak deceit you cause to disappear.
The man who does bloody deeds and deceives is disgusting to YOU.

Translator's note: The author's choices are (1) the *Einheitsübersetzung,* the common translation adopted by contemporary German churches, (2) the original Luther version, (3) the revised Luther version of 1984 (when different from 2), and (4) Martin Buber's translation. For the English translations, I have chosen to use (1) the NRSV, as the nearest functional equivalent of the *Einheitsübersetzung,* with (2), (3), and (4) in my own English approximations of the German originals.

Example Two: Psalm 41:11–12

(NRSV 41:10–11)

But you, O LORD, be gracious to me,
    and raise me up, that I may repay them.
By this I know that you are pleased with me;
    because my enemy has not triumphed over me.

(Unrevised Luther version)

But you, O LORD, be gracious to me and help me,
    thus I will pay them.
By this I see that you are pleased with me,
    that my enemy will not exult over me.

(Revised Luther version)

But you, O LORD, be gracious to me and help me,
    thus I will repay them.
By this I see that you are pleased with me,
    that my enemy will not rejoice over me.

(Martin Buber)

"But you, YOU, lend me favor!
raise me up, that I may pay them!"
By this I have known that you take pleasure in me:
that my enemy cannot rejoice over me.

Example Three: Psalm 58:7–12

(NRSV 58:6–11)

O God, break the teeth in their mouths;
    tear out the fangs of the young lions, O LORD!
Let them vanish like water that runs away;
    like grass let them be trodden down and wither.
Let them be like the snail that dissolves into slime;
    like the untimely birth that never sees the sun.
Sooner than your pots can feel the heat of thorns,
    whether green or ablaze, may he sweep them away!
The righteous will rejoice when they see vengeance done;
    they will bathe their feet in the blood of the wicked.
People will say, "Surely there is a reward for the righteous;
    surely there is a God who judges on earth."

(Unrevised Luther version)

God, break their teeth in their muzzle;
    smash, O LORD, the fangs of the young lions!

They will vanish like water that flows away.
  They aim their arrows; but they shatter.
They disappear like dried-up snails;
  like the untimely birth of a woman, they do not see the sun.
Before your thorns ripen on the thornbush,
  wrath will sweep them away while still green.
The righteous will rejoice to see such vengeance,
  and will bathe his feet in the blood of the godless,
so that people will say: "The righteous will enjoy his fruit;
  there is indeed a God who is judge on earth."

(Revised Luther version)

God, break the teeth in their muzzle,
  shatter, O LORD, the fangs of the young lions!
They will vanish like water that flows away,
  when they aim their arrows, they will break them.
They disappear as wax runs away,
  like a miscarriage that does not see the sun.
Before your pots feel the fire from the thorns,
  burning wrath will sweep everything away.
The righteous will rejoice to see such retaliation,
  and will bathe his feet in the blood of the godless;
and people will say: "Indeed, the righteous receives his fruit,
  indeed, God is still judge on earth."

(Martin Buber)

—God, crush the teeth in their mouth,
the fangs of the lions, crack them, YOU!
Let them dissipate like waters that flow away!
—Harness him, how his arrows are clipped!
As the snail melts, so must he, too, melt away!—
Miscarriages of a woman, they will never see the sun!
Before they notice it, your thorns from the bush by the road:
be they freshly green or dry,
already he is blown away.
The one who is preserved shall rejoice,
for he has seen vengeance,
he can bathe his feet in the blood of the wicked.
People will say: "Surely, the fruits are to the one who is preserved,
surely, divinity abides, judging upon the earth."

Example Four: Psalm 79:10–12

(NRSV)

Why should the nations say,
  "Where is their God?"

Let the avenging of the outpoured blood of your servants
    be known among the nations before our eyes.
Let the groans of the prisoners come before you;
    according to your great power preserve those doomed to die.
Return sevenfold into the bosom of our neighbors
    the taunts with which they taunted you, O Lord!

(Unrevised Luther version)

Why do you let the nations say:
    "Where is their God?"
Let the avenging of the blood of your servants that is poured out
    be known among the nations before our eyes.
Let the sighs of the prisoners come before you;
    according to your great arm, preserve the children of death.
And repay our neighbors sevenfold in their bosom
    their abuse, with which, O LORD, they have reviled you.

(Revised Luther version)

Why do you let the nations say:
    "Where is their God?"
Let the retaliation for the blood of your servants that is poured out
    be known among the nations before our eyes.
Let the sighs of the prisoners come before you;
    with your strong arm, preserve the children of death
and repay our neighbors sevenfold on their heads
    their abuse, with which, O LORD, they have reviled you.

(Martin Buber)

Why should the nations of the world say:
"Where is their God?"
Against the nations will be made known before our eyes
the vengeance for the blood of your servants,
that has been scattered.
Let the groans of those in fetters come before your face!
According to the magnitude of your arm,
let the children of death survive!
let return into the bosom of those who live among us
sevenfold the scorn with which they have derided you,
My LORD!

Example Five: Psalm 94:1–2, 22–23

(NRSV)

O LORD, you God of vengeance,
    you God of vengeance, shine forth!
Rise up, O judge of the earth;

give to the proud what they deserve!
But the LORD has become my stronghold,
   and my God the rock of my refuge.
He will repay them for their iniquity
   and wipe them out for their wickedness;
   the LORD our God will wipe them out.

(Unrevised Luther version)

LORD, God to whom vengeance belongs,
   God to whom vengeance belongs, appear!
Rise up, you judge of the world;
   repay the arrogant as they deserve!
But the LORD is my shelter;
   my God is the refuge of my confidence.
And he will repay them for their iniquity
   and will wipe them out because of their wickedness;
   the LORD, our God will wipe them out.

(Revised Luther version)

LORD, you God of retaliation,
   you God of retaliation, appear!
Rise up, you judge of the world;
   repay the arrogant as they deserve!
But the LORD is my shelter;
   my God is the refuge of my confidence.
And he will repay them for their iniquity
and wipe them out because of their wickedness;
   the LORD, our God will wipe them out.

(Martin Buber)

God of punishments, YOU!
God of punishments, appear!
Rise up, judge of the earth!
Hand back to the arrogant the ripe fruit [of their deeds]!
But HE will be my eyrie,
my God in the rock of my refuge
He lets their malice fall back upon them,
in their wickedness he silences them,
he silences them, He, our God.

Example Six: Psalm 137:7–9

(NRSV)

Remember, O LORD, against the Edomites
   the day of Jerusalem's fall,
how they said, "Tear it down! Tear it down!

Down to its foundations!"
O daughter Babylon, you devastator!
    Happy shall they be who pay you back
        what you have done to us!
Happy shall they be who take your little ones
    and dash them against the rock!

(Unrevised Luther version)

LORD, remember of the children of Edom the day of Jerusalem,
    when they said: "Down with it, down with it to the ground!"
You wretched daughter Babylon,
    happy the one who pays you back what you have done to us!
Happy the one who takes your little children
    and smashes them on a stone!

(Revised Luther version)

LORD, do not forget the sons of Edom, what they said on the day of
Jerusalem:
    "Tear it down! Tear it down to the ground!"
Daughter Babylon, you ravager,
    happy the one who pays you back what you have done to us!
Happy the one who takes your little children
    and smashes them on the rock!

(Martin Buber)

Remember the sons of Edom, YOU,
the day of Jerusalem,
who said: "Lay it bare,
lay what is in her bare, down to the ground!"
Daughter Babylon, ravisher!
Happy the one who pays you
your own deeds, what you did to us:
Happy the one who grabs and smashes
your children on the stones.

Example Seven: Psalm 139:19–22

(NRSV)

O that you would kill the wicked, O God,
    and that the bloodthirsty would depart from me—
those who speak of you maliciously,
    and lift themselves up against you for evil!
Do I not hate those who hate you, O LORD?
    And do I not loathe those who rise up against you?
I hate them with perfect hatred;
    I count them my enemies.

(Unrevised Luther version)

O God, that you would kill the godless,
   and that the bloodthirsty would turn away before me!
For they speak blasphemies of you,
   and your enemies arise without cause.
Indeed, LORD, I hate those who hate you,
   and I loathe those who oppose you.
I hate them to the utmost extent;
   they have become my enemies.

(Revised Luther version)

O God, if only you would kill the godless!
   That the bloodthirsty would turn away from me!
For they speak blasphemously of you,
   and your enemies arise with a saucy spirit.
Should I not hate, LORD, those who hate you,
   and despise those who arise against you?
I hate them to the utmost;
   they have become my enemies.

(Martin Buber)

O God, that you would execute the wicked:
"You men of blood, turn away from me!"
those who hatch plots against you,
your opponents, who exalt themselves to madness!
Do I not hate those who hate you, YOU,
am I not disgusted at those who stand against you?
I hate them with the fullness of hatred,
they have become my enemies.

The Constant Presence of Enemies
throughout the Book of Psalms

It is not just a few psalms that have a repellent effect on many people: the book of Psalms as a whole appears rather unattractive because of its obsession with enemies and violence.

What is the basic model of human life that imbues the quoted examples from the psalms, and the book of Psalms as a whole? Here the life of the individual and of the people Israel appears overwhelmingly to be a daily struggle, an ongoing battle against enemies. The people who pray the psalms feel themselves surrounded, threatened, and shot at by a gigantic army; or they are like an animal pursued by hunters and trappers; or they see themselves surrounded and attacked by rapacious wild beasts, trampling bulls, or poisonous snakes. Even in psalms that express a lyrical underlying mood of confidence and trust, or a joyous harmony with life, there are sudden eruptions of shrill disharmony, recalling enmity, persecution, and hatred.

If one freely and openly admits the emotions and associations that arise on reading or hearing these sections from the psalms, what one feels are irritation and resistance. Even when, most often, the context depicted or envisioned is a juridical one, we are surprised at how violent, destructive, and vengeful this God of the First Testament appears to be. And not only that: Those who pray desire to see and experience the destruction of their enemies and those of their God. It seems to be a question here, not of overcoming feelings of hatred and vengeance, but of intensifying them. The imagery stirs up the potential for aggression and produces fantasies of enmity where, in fact, a judicious distancing is what is really called for. Is it not the fact that here faith in God becomes a weapon against enemies and a legitimation of antagonistic relationships, because those praying are themselves incapable of other kinds of relationships? Is it not the case that here a divine conflict is evoked, and a solution demanded from a God of violence, a God of vengeance, because human beings—for whatever reason—are incapable of conflict *and* of reconciliation?

Who is not repelled by the warlike and aggressive mood of Psalm 8:2 (which was already softened by the Greek translation of the psalm; this milder version migrated thence into the New Testament and Christian translations: cf. Matt. 21:16)—to the extent that one is aware of the contrast to the hymnic praise of the kindness of YHWH the ruler of the world, who cares tenderly for each of YHWH's "human children":

> O LORD, our Sovereign [there is no other!],
>   how majestic is your name in all the earth!
> You have set your glory above the heavens.
>   Out of the mouths of babes and infants
> you have founded a bulwark because of your foes,
>   to silence [make an end to] the enemy and the avenger.
> When I look at your heavens, the work of your fingers,
>   the moon and the stars that you have established;
>   [I am moved to ask:]
> what are human beings that you are mindful of them,
>   mortals that you care for them?
>   (Ps. 8:1–4, NRSV)

And who is not disappointed that the intimate Psalm 23, of which the philosopher Immanuel Kant said, "Not all the books I have read have given me the comfort I received from this word of the Bible," evidently can only project its vision of a mystical communion with God in terms of the pride of victory over a hostile world, and in the knowledge of the fear-inspiring rod that lurks in the background:

> Even though I walk through the
> > darkest valley,
> > I fear no evil;
> for you are with me;
> > your rod and your staff—
> > they comfort me.
> You prepare a table before me
> > in the presence of my enemies.
> > > (Ps. 23:4–5, NRSV)

Once we are sensitized to the "omnipresence" of enemies, enemy imagery, and fear of foes, we are no longer surprised that the "reign of God psalm" 145, so closely aligned with Jesus' "Our Father" and the Kaddish prayer of his time, concludes with the triumphant-sounding assurance:

> The LORD watches over all who
> > love him,
> but all the wicked he will
> > destroy.
> > > (Ps. 145:20, NRSV)

> HE protects all who love him,
> > but he exterminates the wicked.
> > > (Ps. 145:20, Martin Buber)

Those who permit the images, scenes, and life contexts of the individual psalms to affect them will be shocked that there is so much outcry *against* violence, but also so much shrieking *for* violence—and especially at the hope that there is a God of retaliation, vengeance, and destruction.

Those whose roots are in the harmonic, over-affirming, and catechism-style language of Christian prayer literature are surprised by the emotional, concrete, and combative language of most of the psalms; they may be irritated and repelled. It is true that the psalter is saturated with the great theological traditions and themes of the Torah and of prophecy—one could even call it the prayerful acceptance of the Torah and the prophets. But how impiously it is done! This meditation does not take place in the mystical half-light of a gothic cathedral, or in the well-ordered psalmody of monastic oases, or in the silent chambers of the soul: instead, it happens *in the midst of* a world that is often felt to be hostile, *in the midst of* enemies, against whom those at prayer are defending themselves, not least by bringing God forward as their protector and companion in battle.

Norbert Lohfink has put it most succinctly: "The one praying and his or her enemies—that, in short, is the dominant theme of the psalter."[2] There is no complex of words in the psalter that is as plastic and many-faceted as the one that describes enemies. Othmar Keel, in his monograph *Feinde und Gottesleugner. Studien zum Image der Widersacher in den Individualpsalmen,* lists ninety-four (!) words descriptive of enemies.[3] No less rich in variety are the metaphors and comparisons with which God's angry judgment on the enemies of the one praying and the nations hostile to Israel ("Gentiles") are invoked. And when one attempts to understand the book of Psalms, in a synchronic analysis, as a narrative project for life and its world context, the result is the story of a dramatic conflict between the righteous and the wicked—or, in other terms, between the powerless poor and the too-powerful rich—but also between Israel, the people of God, and the idolatrous nations of the earth. That this conflict is ultimately to be decided by the "God of vengeance" who fights on the side of the righteous/poor/Israel is the *basso ostinato* that (sometimes *piano,* sometimes *fortissimo*) joins together all the individual psalms and psalm-songs.

Psalms 1 and 2, as a double motto for the psalter, make us aware that there is a life-and-death struggle going on in the psalms, and the music they are playing is not in a sweet major key. Here we can read, among other lines (in the unrevised Luther version):

But the godless are not so,
    they are like chaff that the wind scatters.
Therefore the godless will not stand in the judgment,
    nor sinners in the congregation of the righteous.
For the LORD knows the way of the righteous;
    but the way of the godless perishes.
                                    (Ps. 1:4–6)

I will preach what the LORD said to me about the wise one:
    "You are my son, today I have begotten you;
ask of me, and I will give you the Gentiles as your heritage
    and the ends of the earth as your possession.
You shall smash them with an iron scepter;
    like clay pots shall you shatter them."
                                    (Ps. 2:7–9)

And before the psalter concludes with the great final "alleluia" of Psalm 150, the "new song" of the victory of God and God's people is sung in Psalm 149 in words and motifs that take up and "fulfill" Psalm 2:[4]

Let the faithful exult in glory;
    let them sing for joy on their couches.
Let the high praises of God be in their throats

and two-edged swords in their hands,
to execute vengeance on the nations
    and punishment on the peoples,
to bind their kings with fetters
    and their nobles with chains of iron,
to execute on them the judgment decreed.
    This is glory for all his faithful ones.
Praise the LORD!

(Ps. 149:5–9, NRSV)

In fact, hatred, enmity, violence, retaliation, and even revenge are not sub-motifs in the psalter: they are substantive parts of it. Thus we can scarcely be surprised that the psalms and their image of God have aroused resistance and rejection in Christian theology and psychology, sometimes even leading to rejection of the Old Testament and of the Bible as a whole.

Protest and Rejection in the Name of Christianity

The complexity and depth of the theological difficulty created by the psalms for a great many Christian theologians is evident, in the first place, from the numerous statements on this subject in recent years.

The fundamental hermeneutical problem erupts most harshly when the psalms are interpreted as texts created in pre-Christian Judaism, and when strong emphasis is laid on the discontinuity between Judaism and Christianity. In such cases, the psalter is somehow made to stand before the judgment seat of New Testament christology and ecclesiology, there to be "Christianized" or even rejected as partly "unchristian."

Balthasar Fischer, a liturgical scholar from Trier, gives this reason for saying that the psalter must be "Christianized" before it can be admitted as Christian prayer:

> What is good about the psalms is that they are so human. . . . A certain difficulty arises from the fact that these songs . . . come from the Old Testament; thus they were written before the coming of Christ, and only in rare instances do they refer to the coming Messiah. How can they be made Christian prayer, in which Christ is the center, whether we are praying to him directly or uniting ourselves with him in prayer[?][5]

In this case, the problem of the psalms of enmity, vengeance, and cursing is not considered as a *fundamental* problem of the intersection of religion and violence, and not even as a difficulty within the Jewish tradition, which of course speaks not *only* about a "God of vengeance," but also about a "God of forgiveness and love." In most christologies, these psalms are "pre-Christian" relics; they are "unchristian" or "less than Christian," that is, typical of the Old Testament and of Judaism, and they reflect a type of piety that Christians *as Christians* must overcome and leave behind them. It is perfectly obvious to me that this is a survival of the thesis propagated in the second century by Marcion, the bishop's son who was condemned as a heretic: namely, that of an opposition between the God of Judaism (that is, of the Old Testament) and the very different God of Jesus Christ.

However, this observation by no means simplifies the problem, for there are more than a few Christian Old Testament scholars who describe the problematic passages in the psalms as "less than Christian," or typical of the Old Testament, as the rather random sampling below will demonstrate.

In an essay titled "Heute christlich Psalmen beten [Praying the Psalms as a Christian Today]," Alfred Mertens, Old Testament scholar from Mainz, gives a very sensitive introduction to praying the psalms, and yet concludes:

> Ultimately, of course, Christians at prayer will keep in mind that, in praying [the psalms] they find themselves within a pre-Christian and sub-Christian ethos, on a level far surpassed by the Sermon on the Mount.[6]

From among the exegetical commentaries, I have chosen the commentaries on Psalms by Bernhard Duhm[7] and Artur Weiser,[8] because Christian prejudice runs like a red thread almost throughout these books. Thus Duhm writes:

> Although the simple truth of the poem attracts us, for Christian sensibilities the attitude to enemies is alienating [p. 22, Psalm 6]. . . . and for a Christian view of the world and of life, its naive joy . . . cannot quite satisfy [p. 46, Psalm 16].
> Its ideas of suffering, sin, and happiness are less than Christian [p. 95, Psalm 32].
> Even the "depth" of the consciousness of sin is not really Christian [p. 148, Psalm 51].
> The curses in this psalm are to a particular degree "unchristian;" nevertheless it has been considered messianic (even in Acts 1:16–20) [p. 254, Psalm 109].

In Artur Weiser's commentary on Psalms we read:

> we must nevertheless not overlook the fact that it is precisely that superficial mechanical conception of the working of God's righteousness which erected a barrier strong enough to prevent the psalmist from pressing on towards love as the deepest motive power for moral action and from recognizing his neighbour in anyone who is in need of help. It is for this reason that on this point the psalm does not go beyond that barrier, which has been surmounted in the New Testament [p. 170, Psalm 15]. . . .

The psalmist's hope of being able to requite his adversaries for what they have done to him is indeed understandable, arising, as it does, out of his indignation and disappointment, but clearly shows that in this passage, under the judgment of the New Testament, Old Testament thought is restricted by emotions which are far too human [p. 345, Psalm 41].

The psalm shows its limitations clearly. We have no right to doubt the subjective sincerity of its author; his trust in the divine faithfulness and help . . . does not lack power. The worshipper is, however, neither able nor ready to give himself up wholly to God, trusting [God] absolutely, and accept his suffering from [God's] hand, enduring it patiently. Human self-will and [human] low instincts of vindictiveness and gloating retain their power over his thoughts and affect also his idea of God and his relationship to [God]. . . . This is why the worshipper's prayer is also unable to exercise a liberating influence; for it does not lead on to the uttermost depths of ultimate truth. In this respect the prayer is subject to the judgment of the New Testament [pp. 416–417, Psalm 54]. . . .

The psalm's conclusion, speaking of the effect of the judgment on the righteous, shows on the other hand the undisguised gloating and the cruel vindictiveness of an intolerant religious fanaticism (cf. Ps. 68:23); it is one of those dangerous poisonous blossoms which are liable to grow even on the tree of religious knowledge and clearly show the limits set to the Old Testament religion [p. 432, Psalm 58].

The hymn is a sturdy comrade; its boldness and unbroken courageous testimony to God have already enabled many a [person] to overcome all sorts of temptations. . . . True, the Christian's trust in God requires a further readiness to submit to God's will, even when [God] has resolved to deal with us in ways other than those we expected the venture of faith to take [p. 613, Psalm 91].

It is because they are God's enemies that they are also [the author's] enemies. Though we can fully understand such motives of hatred which do not spring from the lower sphere of sentiments that are far too human, we must, however, not overlook the fact that the poet here actually stops at the limits set by Old Testament tradition [p. 807, Psalm 139].

It is undeniable that this kind of labeling of the irritating psalms or psalm verses makes the unquestionable starting point for all judgments the centuries-long Christian tradition according to which the New Testament per se always represents the privileged forum that demonstrates the limitations of the Old Testament (cf. Weiser's stereotyping).

With that as a starting point, one is unexpectedly confronted by the question whether these psalms are at all appropriate as Christian prayer, or at least whether they must not be revised and rephrased in a Christian sense.

That is the position taken by Otto Knoch, New Testament professor from Passau and former director of the Catholic Bible Society (Katholisches Bibelwerk).

> Can a Christian, as a member of the new people of God, pray all the psalms in just the same way as a Jew, a member of the old people of God, or does the new order of salvation and the orientation of the Christian to Jesus Christ, the risen Lord of the church and humanity, demand an alteration of the psalm texts and the way of praying the psalms? . . .
> Through Jesus of Nazareth, the Christ, God is definitively revealed and has reconciled the world to himself (cf. 2 Cor. 5:11–19). As a member of the body of Christ, who through baptism has entered into a new life-relationship with Christ and thus with God, the Christian prays. . . .
> Thus the Christian, like the church, prays "in, with, and through Jesus Christ" to God the Father. Therefore the prayers of the Old Testament are to be clarified and unlocked on the basis of his message and teaching. . . .
> There is need for an examination and more profound interpretation of the psalms of the old covenant in terms of Jesus Christ, the church, and the reign of God. That is why the Catholic church, both in the missal and in the Liturgy of the Hours, has removed the psalms and sections of psalms that call for vengeance and retribution, as well as those that clearly betray Old Testament-Jewish ideas; in addition, by means of introductory verses and prayers, all the psalms and portions of psalms have been ordered within the context of the Christian history of salvation and the church's prayer.[9]

It is undeniable that the object in taking such a stance is, on the one hand, the "rescuing" of the biblical psalms for Christianity. This position aims to avoid the general heresy of Marcion, and yet it partially preserves it. The annoying strangeness of the psalms is attributed to their "less than Christian" Jewish origins, in order that the newness and superiority of Christianity may appear all the more luminous. Thus the psalms of vengeance become a foil for contrast with the new gospel. They make it obvious to us why Christ had to come.

This is evident, with all its consequences and pungent effect, in those authors who regard these psalms, as symptoms and elements of Old Testament religion, as something deeply "alien" in relationship to Christianity. In this connection, the voices of those who want to follow Marcion in eliminating the Old Testament from the Christian canon are not so important. The theological problem of the "psalms of violence" has its full impact where there is an attempt to reconcile the (real or supposed) alien feeling of these psalms with their canonical and biblical quality by granting some positive function to their very strangeness. This usually is accomplished by use of an underlying dialectic metaphor that appears in several variations.

In 1962, during the discussions of the reform of the Catholic church's Liturgy of the Hours, the Benedictine Abbot Primate Benno Gut, who in 1969 would become prefect of the new Sacred Congregation for Divine Worship, responded in the Central Commission of the Vatican Council to the question whether the so-called imprecatory psalms would be retained or eliminated by saying, "In spite of these important negative votes, let me be permitted to defend the imprecatory psalms, so that through them our consciousness may be repeatedly awakened, and that we may be grateful to God for the marvelous development of divine revelation."[10] Heinrich Junker, professor of Old Testament at Trier, had described the role of the imprecatory psalms in religious pedagogy in much the same way in 1940:

> In conclusion, let me simply attempt a brief answer to the question: "How can we really pray those psalms today, if we can no longer truly accept their genuine meaning at every point?" In responding, I will set aside any metaphorical interpretations of the text, and presume worshipers who, for example, understand these psalms . . . in the sense originally intended. If they come across passages that, in terms of Christian morality, they cannot accept, they will call to mind, from their Christian knowledge, the New Testament corrective to this imperfect Old Testament way of thinking. Indeed, mature and enlightened worshipers will accomplish this correction of the Old Testament prayers without pride or irreverent criticism, for they know that they, as human beings, are not on a higher moral plane than the Old Testament worshiper: honest self-knowledge tells them that they too, if put to a serious test, could at any moment succumb to the temptation to utter vengeful prayers. The only advantage they have over Old Testament worshipers is that they have been shown a higher ideal and a more sublime commandment.[11]

The "strangeness" of the Old Testament in contrast to the message of the justifying grace of the New Testament became, in reality, a dialectical principle of Lutheran dogmatic theology for a whole series of influential authors, from Emanuel Hirsch (1888–1972) and Friedrich Baumgärtel (1888–1981) to Franz Hesse (emeritus professor of Old Testament at Münster). They have in common an adherence to the canonical Old Testament and its salvific significance for Christians as well, although *e contrario*—that is, according to them Christians discover in the Old Testament the "old" human being also present in themselves as long as and whenever they do not believe in the message of Christ. Most of the psalms as well, especially those that call on God in full confidence to exercise judgment on enemies, are seen as testimony to the "alien religion" from which Jesus wishes to deliver us.

Emanuel Hirsch, the son of a Lutheran pastor, was born in Wittenberg. Among his teachers was the "Marcionite" Adolf von Harnack. Hirsch himself, as a professor at Göttingen, exercised great influence in the realm of scholarly politics, and finally, in 1933, he joined the church movement of "German Christians" and took an active part in the persecution of Jews. However, none of this dispenses us from listening to the serious questions raised by Hirsch, at the very beginning of his theological career, about the Christian relevance of the psalms. Hirsch was probably moved in part by his theologically and politically motivated hatred of Jews to propose the thesis that the Old Testament "has been abolished and destroyed for us by faith in Jesus,"[12] but also in part by an experience of the psalms that he himself relates:

> I preached less frequently from the Old Testament than many of our ministers at that time. However, on the celebrations of the great turning points, when the object was to teach how God's working in the history of the nations can be courageously accepted by an obedient and submissive faith, it seemed to me the most natural thing. I chose passages that expressed those things in the Old Testament faith in God as the lord of history that remained true for Christians, and attempted to make them contemporary. This caused me no difficulty of conscience: what was important was the choice of passages and the appropriate definition of the purpose of the sermon.
>
> Ultimately, the ease of this way of preaching concealed from me for a long time how difficult it can be for preachers and pastors to make a proper Christian use of the Old Testament. The difficulties of their profession, which can only be discovered by years of experience, were not vivid for me, who had chosen a scholarly career. Another difficult experience, however, came to my aid. During the time when I was active in preaching, I frequently read from the psalter while visiting the sick (somewhat in the spirit expressed in Luther's famous prefatory remarks on the psalter, which had always been very dear to me). So, one day, I was reading from the ninety-first Psalm for a rather poor and deeply despondent village woman, the mother of a son who was at the front. Seldom have I seen such deep devotion and such blessed consolation come over a human being as I did then. When I came back a few days later, the woman was up and about, but she wanted to hear a psalm read. I began another one, but she asked for the one she had heard before. When I asked her why, I made the hideous discovery of the source of her deep devotion and consolation. "A thousand may fall at your side, ten thousand at your right hand, but it will not come near you"—this she had taken as a personal oracle promising that God would bring her son back alive; unlike so many others about her, in the village and the city, who had lost or would lose their husbands or sons, she would keep hers. I attempted, as kindly as possible, to help her to under-

stand that this was not a Christian way of trusting in God. She re-
acted with hostile rejection, and pastoral access to her heart remained closed to me forever. As I returned home, having helped a
human being to learn a false belief and unable to repair the harm,
the thought leapt into my head: "The woman was in some sense
quite right! Her faith was just like that of the psalm you read to her!"
Since then I have avoided this psalm in Christian pastoral work and
instruction. But I became very reserved in the use of the Old Testament psalter in general, at the sickbed and in the classroom. I pre-
ferred to read something from the New Testament, or from our
German Protestant psalter, the hymnbook. For at that time, slowly
but with an amazing violence, first the psalms and later other parts
of the Old Testament began to reveal to me their Old Testament-
Jewish face, so alien to Christianity.[13]

This key experience in Schopfheim in Baden no doubt drew together a
whole set of Hirsch's unresolved problems, especially his opinion that the
First World War was lost by the Germans because of the absence of a national will to sacrifice (a lack he saw in the sick woman, and which he also
considered the typical attitude of the German Jews!). But his question, how
certain passages in the psalms could be understood and prayed as authentic prayers of faith, again reveals the complexity of the problem, although
it calls for a different solution than that given by Hirsch, and adopted and
defended by Friedrich Baumgärtel and his student, Franz Hesse.

Baumgärtel in particular sharpened Hirsch's thesis, according to which
the Christian significance of the Jewish Old Testament consists in its revelation to us of the resistance that struggles in us against the gospel, and particularly in uncovering the "Old Testament devotee in us" who needs "to be
uplifted . . . into what is Christian."[14] Baumgärtel wrote:

> As Christians, we have a gloriously free path to communion with our
> God, and yet we are fettered, just as were the worshipers in the Old
> Testament. . . . Thus, as Christians, we stand in the midst of the Old
> Testament and strive, like the Old Testament and with it, to rise up
> into the New Testament.[15]

Thus the pedagogical function of the Old Testament for salvation, including that of the psalms, consists in its setting evil before our eyes and awak-
ening in us the desire for the salvation that comes to us *only* from listening
to the New Testament. In the psalms, we can learn what God is *not*.
Baumgärtel said this with special emphasis about the so-called messianic
psalms, whose violent king (cf. Ps. 2:9; 110:5–7) is certainly not the true Mes-
siah, whom God showed and sent to us in Jesus Christ:

> These messianic psalms ultimately speak of a redeemer king who
> comes, and whose *doxa* [glory] is already hidden in the present

king. In his ultimate coming he will realize what the poets apply to
the empirical king as the meaning of his office: the accomplishment
of political and social integration. But these redeemer hymns miss
the truth of the redeemer whom the Christian community sees and
confesses. His *doxa* is the power to forgive sins, and his saving work
for lost humanity realized in his death and resurrection.[16]

Baumgärtel intensifies this still further: Because Jesus was the opposite of
the hopes aroused by the messianic psalms, "he had to die for it"! Jesus desires to liberate us from the false hopes of these psalms, which repeatedly
arise in us as "Old Testament" people. To understand *this* mission of his, we
require a confrontation with the seductive *Fata Morgana* of these psalms:

> The theological interpretation of these psalms is only possible *e con-*
> *trario,* as contrasting parallels to the New Testament message. This
> contrasting parallelism does very effective service in the proclama-
> tion of the Gospel: It is a warning signal for Christians not to cou-
> ple their faith with a desire for national and political integration
> and the integration of society.[17]

Less dogmatic, but ultimately more serious, are the objections to the
psalms of enmity that arise from pastoral experiences and suggestions. Even
if we must diagnose the objections of some pastors that these psalms full of
hatred and violence are simply no longer acceptable to people today, with
their sensitivity to violence in the cloak of religion, as at least in part the
problems of the pastors themselves, they indicate a further dimension of
the problem presented by these psalms. In principle, it is a good thing that
the fundamentalist naiveté with which every liturgical text used to be accepted more or less unthinkingly because it was "sacred" or "the word of
God" has, for the most part, disappeared—but it also demands that we deal
with texts that are found to be difficult. In another chapter, we will say something about why "pastoral acceptability" cannot be an exclusive criterion.
But it is not our business simply to set aside all pastoral considerations.

In the 1980 issue of *Bibel und Kirche* titled "Wie Psalmen heute beten?
[How Can We Pray the Psalms Today?]," Gemma Hinricher, prioress of the
Carmelite convent at Dachau, reports in part as follows on her experiences
with praying the psalms:

> As early as 1965 we received permission to pray the Office in the ver-
> nacular. However, this vernacular prayer, which had become nec-
> essary and requisite for the sake of the tourists, also brought with it
> serious problems for our recitation of prayer in choir, because of
> the so-called imprecatory or vengeance psalms, and the cursing pas-
> sages in a number of psalms. We were soon tempted to return to
> Latin, for no matter how much the vernacular brought home to us
> the riches of the psalms, the Latin had at least covered up the weak-

nesses of the psalms as prayer. In the immediate *vicinity of the concentration camp,* we felt ourselves unable to say out loud psalms that spoke of a punishing, angry God and of the destruction of enemies, often in hideous images, and whose content was the desire for destruction and vengeance, in the presence of people who came into our church agitated and mentally distressed by their visit to the camp. It often happens that these people are not only moved by the hideousness and brutality they encounter in the documentation in the concentration camp museum and in viewing the camp itself, but also by their own feelings of hatred and revenge because of the dreadful thing that happened in this place. Our church is the only calming influence in the camp compound. Tourists, after visiting the camp, pass through the north watchtower into the courtyard in front of the church and convent. Many of them pause, and seek to find some inner peace in our church. It is probably understandable that neither verses nor whole psalms of cursing, neither desires for destruction nor for vengeance can be uttered in the midst of such a stillness.

Our prayer should be such that it can encourage people to reconciliation, forgiveness, and love. It should be such that the presence of God can be experienced: "Where two or three are gathered in my name, I am there among them" (Matt. 18:20). In our praying and singing together, Jesus Christ is experienced as present, as the loving one whose reconciling and forgiving love overcame hatred.

So it was clear to us that, for us today, all the biblical-theological, literary, and hermeneutical objections to the elimination of cursing psalms and passages were of no avail. For us here, pastoral service to people who visit this place and this church comes first. The Office is a service; certainly it is divine service primarily, but at the same time it is also a service for people, and carrying out that service to the fullest is the duty of a community that prays the Liturgy of the Hours.[18]

The prioress addresses still another problem that is worthy of reflection:

It is a different matter whether one prays the Liturgy of the Hours privately or in community. There are certain criteria for common prayer that simply must be fulfilled. If prayer texts are spoken in common, it must also be possible to perform them in common. A prayer spoken aloud has its own rules. There are certain limits to the performance of texts whose content is sensed and experienced quite differently in common prayer than when they are recited privately. Psalms and verses that curse can "disappear," or be ignored in private prayer. One can be sustained by an antiphon, and one can more easily harmonize the biblical-theological interpretation of a psalm with one's personal prayer than is possible in a common recitation of the psalms. We may suspect that many of those who de-

fend the psalms and passages of cursing do not recite the Liturgy of
the Hours in common, at least not in the vernacular. Calls for
vengeance and destruction, and similar utterances, are unbearable
in public utterance, and for those who pray the psalms together out
loud. Even if one is acquainted with biblical theology, it is not always
possible to file the offensive verses in the correct biblical-theological categories. At any rate, the texts of cursing and calls for
vengeance also introduce special psychological difficulties when
there is prayer in common.[19]

Objection in the Name of a Humane Ethics

Probably the most severe objection to the psalms was raised in 1992 by
Franz Buggle, a clinical psychologist from Freiburg, in his book, *Denn sie wissen nicht, was sie glauben. Oder warum man redlicherweise nicht mehr Christ sein
kann. Eine Streitschrift.* In support of his thesis that the whole Bible, including both the Old and New Testaments, is in its essential parts an utterly violent and inhuman book, and therefore must be rejected—in fact, actively
opposed—as the basis for a responsible ethics today, he brings forward numerous observations and arguments based on the book of Psalms. Against
the widespread admiration for the psalms, he unequivocally states:

> [This is] what the psalms really are: in large part, and to a degree
> seldom encountered otherwise, a text dominated by primitive and
> uncontrolled feelings of hatred, desire for vengeance, and self-
> righteousness. . . . In spite of all apparent "matters of fact" that seem
> to deny it, I must acknowledge that for a long time I have not read
> any text so marked by excessive and unbridled hatred and thirst for
> revenge.[20]

According to Buggle, anyone who reads the psalms without prejudice,
who does not theologically gloss over the violent, destructive, and irrational
images of God expressed in them, or minimize the eruptions of vengeful
hatred and the arrogance of the egocentric self-righteousness of the one
praying the psalms by means of "solemn" veneration, can only be shocked
to the core by the theologically legitimated and ecclesiastically propagated
spirit of enmity and the glorification of violence found here. Therefore he
concludes:

> Should it not gradually become clear to everyone that the really se-
> rious objections to the Bible are not so much anthropological in na-
> ture? That God did not create the world in seven days, or whether
> the sun stood still or not—these are scarcely the problems we have
> with the Bible today. Here the battle is often being carried on
> against substitute arguments, "straw figures." Instead, that the ethi-

cal and moral level of the biblical God, who is supposed to be the embodiment of the most high God, is found to be so archaically inhuman in many of his statements that it would not be difficult for anyone living today to name a whole crowd of *people* he or she knows whose ethical and moral level, despite all their obvious weaknesses and failures, would be far above that of the biblical God: *that* is the essential objection, and it is clear that it is nourished not only by the Bible, which in large measure *correctly reflects* the partly hideous and inhuman reality, even though it *interprets* it *inhumanly and archaically* (suffering and evil as God's punishment, etc.). It is nourished equally by the fact of the endlessly real and current suffering of creatures in light of the assertion that there exists, at the same time, an all-powerful, all-knowing, good God who embodies endless love itself: This is the ancient problem of theodicy, which the churches and other theistic apologists even today suppress, but do not solve.[21]

Because the psalms continue to be used in the liturgy, and especially in the Liturgy of the Hours, this destructive and ethically perverse image of God can go on working without hindrance, according to Buggle. The ethical deformation accomplished by the violence-obsessed and violence-propagating book of Psalms is dangerous above all, he believes, because the psalter not only enjoys the highest veneration within the church, but "even in groups that regard themselves as rather liberal and enlightened, the psalter is seen as one of the largely unquestioned pluses of biblical and Christian religious conviction."[22]

2

A Look at the Psalms Themselves

Before we attempt a systematic sketch of the hermeneutical and biblical-theological horizons within which the psalms of enmity were originally intended to be seen and heard (cf. chapter 3), we need to choose some psalm texts from which we can derive a series of observations regarding the profile, intention, and function of the violence-laden image of God that shapes these psalms. We will adhere to the hermeneutical option on which we have already insisted: Difficult, awkward, and resistant texts must first of all be perceived and taken seriously in their resistant nature. A foreignness sensed within a text may not be charged against it *a priori*, causing it to be too quickly condemned and rejected before it has a chance to make its whole case. The fundamental rule for all communication also applies in the encounter with these psalms we find so difficult: Dialogue partners must be taken seriously if we want to understand and communicate with them, even if it be to disagree with them. Thus those who are prepared to expose themselves to the foreignness of the "violent psalms" must also confront the question whether this foreignness is not primarily within themselves. This could be the beginning of a lively struggle with the text, leading to a friendship that changes and shapes the readers themselves. It could happen that the readers of these psalms, in attempting to understand the text, will suddenly acquire new insights into themselves, the world in which they live, and even God. Without jumping into the conversation too quickly, without shoving them aside in know-it-all fashion, without expressing judgment out of a sense of Christian superiority, we need to try to understand these texts in their historical context, their linguistic shape, and their theological passion. That is the first task.

I have chosen seven psalms with which to illustrate, at least selectively, the multiple perspectives involved in speaking of the God of vengeance and violence in the book of Psalms. Among the group are all three of the psalms that have been entirely omitted from the Roman Catholic church's Liturgy of the Hours (Pss. 58, 83, and 109). Out of the group of nineteen psalms from which ecclesiastical censorship has dropped individual verses, I have chosen Psalms 137 and 139. I add Psalms 12 and 44 because we can see in them how Israel had already stated and refined the problem of perspectives on violence.

I will present each text in my own working translation, the details of which, of course, I cannot explicate here. Unfortunately, an extensive analysis and interpretation of the psalms is impossible. I will attempt to present the points of view that are significant for the theme at hand.

Psalm 12: Protest against the Violence of Violent People*

1   For the choir leader. On the Sheminith. A Psalm of David.
2a   Rescue [me], YHWH, for the godly are in dire straits,
2b   the faithful have disappeared from humankind.
3a   They speak lies to each other,
3b   with smooth lips and a double heart they speak.

4a   May YHWH root out all smooth lips,
4b   the tongue that makes such boasts,
5a   those who say, "With our tongues we are powerful,
5b   if our lips are with us, who is lord over us?"

6a   "Because of the rape of the oppressed, because of the groans of the poor,
6b   now I will arise," says YHWH,
6c   "I will bring rescue to the one against whom they are snorting!"

7a   The words of YHWH are pure words,
7b   refined silver, smelted in the furnace, purified seven times.

8a   You, YHWH, will protect them,
8b   you will guard them from this generation forever,
9a   even though the wicked prowl all around,
9b   even though vileness is great among the children of humankind.

Translator's note: In standard English Bibles, what is here indicated as verse 1 is the heading, and the numbering begins with what is here verse 2, so that all verse numbers in the German edition (and in this translation) are +1 with respect to English.

Psalm 12, probably from just before the exile, was redactionally adapted to Psalm 11 by the addition of verse 9. Its language and theology are inspired by the course of the prophetic liturgies of lament in which, in situations of danger, a "saving" word of God was implored from the mouth of a cultic prophet. The basic structure of such a liturgy of lament had three parts: (1) Outcry over the dangerous or disastrous situation (uttered by the liturgist, accompanied by the congregation's expressions of lament); (2) God's answer in "I" form (uttered by the cultic prophet, here exercising the typical role of the prophet, that is, speaking on behalf of God); (3) Reaction of the congregation to the word of God received (usually praise and thanksgiving, but also expression of confidence and hope). Our psalm is oriented to this schema. It is composed in consistent fashion to culminate in the direct speech of God in verse 6. The concentric structure of the speech-act is easily recognized from the arrangement of the speech-directions: verses 2–3 are "you" addresses to YHWH (with YHWH in the second person); verses 4–5 are a wish/petition to YHWH (with YHWH in the third person); verse 6 is direct speech of God (with YHWH in the first person); verse 7 is a statement about YHWH's word (with YHWH in the third person); verses 8–9 are "you" addresses to YHWH (with YHWH in the second person). The series is thus ABCBA. This concentric pattern is also emphasized by the language itself: The beginning and end are tied together by the key phrase "[children of] humankind," forming an *inclusio*. The divine speech in verse 6, highlighted by its three-part form as the center of the psalm, takes up the first word of the psalm to show that it is the fulfillment of the petition uttered there (v. 2a, "rescue"; v. 6c, "I will rescue"). The psalm uses the divine name, YHWH, five times, once in each of the five sections ABCBA; in this way, verse 6 is again elevated as the center of the psalm.

Thus, as a dynamic linguistic prayer event, the psalm is constructed as follows: It begins with a cry for help, with a twofold foundation and a developed description of the social crisis (vv. 2–3). This is followed by a wish for the elimination of the wicked, whose unbridled arrogance and actual godlessness is given an impressive poetic summary in a quotation (vv. 4–5); the additional quotation of the word of God in verse 6 stands out as a contrast to what had gone before. Verse 7 then responds with praise of the word of God, couched in a nominally hymnic style. The psalm concludes with the confession in verses 8–9, beginning with the emphatic personal pronoun "you." With this confession, the believer opposes the cruelty of the wicked, whose dominance is still being endured in the present, and appeals for resistance to them—motivated by the very power that the recitation of this psalm is meant to give, and can give.

The following observations are important for our particular questions:

1. The psalm presents a massive critique of society in the style of wisdom literature and prophetic analysis. It discloses the destructive misuse of human words that has escalated to a quasi-institutional brutality, and apparently is even regarded as socially legitimate.
2. The psalm does not point either to mythical or demonic powers as causes, but makes individual people and groups of people responsible, naming the roots of their violent actions.
3. The psalm resists any suggestion of a theological legitimation or glossing over of the violence that destroys human lives. Where people are oppressed and violated, God's own truth is at stake.
4. The psalm presents a many-faceted image of God. On the one hand, the plea in verse 4 calls concretely for the destroyer God. On the other hand, the divine promise in verse 6 is formulated in rather general terms, and it emphasizes only the saving aspect. The consoling undertones of divine solidarity with the victims are unmistakable.
5. The word of God does not provoke the violence of the victims against their executioners; the vicious circle of violence is broken here by remembrance of YHWH as the rescuer and protector of the poor. The concluding verse 9 even calls for patience, despite the unrestricted domination of structural violence in society.
6. The psalm reveals different aspects of violence: Against the destructive violence of the wicked it evokes the saving violence of YHWH, which comes to the aid of the poor and the weak in their helplessness and "lifts them up." These two aspects of violence could quite legitimately be distinguished by the two concepts of *violentia* (repressive violence) and *potestas* (legitimate violence), but perhaps they can be qualified even better by a distinction between the ideas of "violence" and "power."[1]

Psalm 139: Passionate Struggle against Structural Violence

1a For the choir leader. A psalm of David.
1b YHWH, you have searched me and known me.
2a You, you yourself know when I sit down and when I rise up,
2b   you have discerned my thoughts from far away.
3a You search out my path and my lying down,
3b   and have watched over all my ways.
4a Even before a word is on my tongue,
4b   see, you know it completely.
5a You hem me in, behind and before,

5b   and you have laid your hand upon me.
6a   Such [your] knowledge is too wonderful for me,
6b   it is so high that I cannot grasp it.

7a   Where can I go from your spirit?
7b   Or where can I flee from your presence?
8a   If I were to ascend to heaven, you are there!
8b   And if I were to make my bed in the underworld, there you are!
9a   If I take the wings of the morning
9b   and settle at the farthest limits of the sea,
10a   even there your hand would lead me,
10b   and your right hand hold me fast.
11a   And I said: "Only darkness shall grasp at me
11b   and the light around me become night!"
12a   But even the darkness is not dark to you
12b   and the night is as bright as the day: for darkness is as light to you.

13a   For it was you who formed my inner organs,
13b   you wove me together in my mother's womb.
14a   I thank you, for I am fearfully and wonderfully made,
14b   wonderful are your works, and this my soul knows very well.
15a   My frame was not hidden from you,
15b   when I was being made in secret.
15c   Intricately was I woven in the depths of the earth,
16a   your eyes beheld my unformed substance.
16b   And in your book were written
16c   all my days, before they were formed, when none of them as yet
            existed!

17a   But how weighty to me are your thoughts,
17b   O God! how vast is the sum of them!
18a   If I tried to count them, they are more than the sand;
18b   if I came to the end, I would still be with you!
19a   O that you would kill the wicked, O God!
19b   "Depart from me, you men of blood!"
20a   They speak of you maliciously,
20b   and lift up your name in vain; they are your adversaries.
21a   Do I not hate those who hate you, YHWH?
21b   And do I not loathe those who rise up against you?
22a   Yes, I hate them with perfect hatred;
22b   I count them my enemies.
23a   Search me, O God, and know my heart!
23b   Test me and know my cares!
24a   See if I am on the way of destruction—
24b   and lead me in the everlasting way.

Is it not understandable, and does it not make sense, that verses 19–22 have been eliminated from this psalm when it is prayed in the Liturgy of the Hours? Even Dorothee Sölle simply drops these verses when she interprets the psalm in her little book, *Die Hinreise*.[2] If we look at the "critical" commentaries, we can find a multitude of arguments for this omission. There are even exegetes who would like to excise verses 19–24 as an independent song, because they do not match the preceding text in verses 1–18: "Can it be," wrote Hans Schmidt, "that these passionately intrusive verses, oddly uneven in their rhythm, really belong to the quiet poem in combination with which we have received them?"[3]

Even as important a student of the psalms as Hermann Gunkel expresses enthusiasm, on the one hand, for the theological profundity of verses 1–18, but registers strong reservations about verses 19–22:

> Our psalmist is the heir of the prophets and lyric poets. He stands astonished before the great mystery that there are no limits to God's knowledge and power. These are ideas that are new and surprising to him; hence the unique, powerful freshness with which he expresses them, and that is also why the psalm is counted as a classic expression of these ideas in Christian communities even to the present day. . . . Just as the creation song in [Psalm] 104 turns at the end (v. 35) to the wicked, who destroy the harmony of God's marvelous world, and expresses the wish that they may be consumed . . . so also with this song. It thrusts at them with enraged passion. . . . It is a remarkable phenomenon that a man who can sink so ardently into the intimacy of God can suddenly re-emerge with such ferocity when he remembers the wicked. But it is a genuinely Israelite picture. This nation with its volatile temperament and passionate subjectivity recognizes, in religion as in all things, only truth and lies; there is nothing in between. Thus it happens that this religion is completely intolerant: There can be no mercy for those with different beliefs; instead, when possible, they should be destroyed! . . . Indeed, the profound meditation of this psalmist and his rage against the arrogant are intimately connected: The same glow of feeling that thrusts him to his knees before the All-One causes him to rage violently against those who do not share his feeling. . . . The saying about the God who lets rain fall on the just and the unjust alike would have been incomprehensible to the people of this age.[4]

Can the "evil" be obviated by simply striking out verses 19–22? The rather common understanding of the psalm that is reflected in the titles given to it in translations of the Bible does, in fact, suggest this solution. Anyone who reads the psalm as a philosophical meditation on the theme of "human beings before the all-knowing God" (the title given it in the German *Einheitsübersetzung*) can easily do without verses 19–22.

However, this psalm is not at all a "hymn to farseeing divine providence, which has ordered everything from the beginning, so that human fate has been known to it from the start."[5] It is the prayer of an individual who, with a positively prophetic passion, wrestles in prayer to work out his or her individual "suffering because of God" who has taken possession of him or her (vv. 1b–6), and from whom he or she cannot escape (vv. 7–12). Anyone who too quickly eliminates verses 19–22 in order to obtain a "beautiful" psalm must also cut out the lamenting and even accusatory undertones that echo already in verses 1–12, where the one praying, like Jeremiah (cf. the confessions in Jer. 12:1–6; 15:10–21; 20:7–18) and Job (cf. especially Job 7:12–21) experiences the presence of God as a burden and an impediment. Those who strike out verses 19–22 because of an excess of "Christian" zeal must be aware that in doing so they are destroying the whole intention of the psalm, both from the poetic and the theological point of view! Moreover, the result of the elimination of verses 19–22 is that the psalm has a positively absurd ending. The plea that God will "test" the one who prays (v. 23ab) is only meaningful in light of the preceding explanation in verses 21–22, according to which the sole concern of the person praying is God's own interest. Similarly, the alternative of the two ways presupposed in verse 24 can only be understood if one already knows of the concrete description of these two ways addressed in verses 19–22.

In this psalm, two superimposed structures shape the dynamic of the prayer.[6] First, there is the frame (*inclusio*) in verses 1a and 23–24, which, with its verbal repetitions, creates a tension between indicative and imperative. In this connection it is important to note that the statement in verse 1b carries something of a negative connotation, as verses 2–12 show (that YHWH has searched the one praying is something that the latter experiences as being seized and made captive—something from which she or he has wanted to escape; in fact, the desire to escape is still present!). On the other hand, the imperatives in verses 23–24 have a positive connotation: YHWH is to see that the one who prays is serious, and ought therefore to come to his or her aid! This framework encloses the principal section with its four divisions: verses 2–6, 7–12, 13–16, 17–22. The four divisions are indicated primarily by their different linguistic structures: verses 2–6 enunciate individual circumstances from the past, relating YHWH's dealing with the one who prays; the address is an emphatic and reproachful "you" (in the familiar second person singular). Verses 7–12 begin with emphatic questions. This section is strongly I-centered; it describes the present situation of the one praying, experienced as the consequence of the divine action described in verses 2–6. Verses 13–16 again refer to a past action of YHWH toward the person now praying, and again the emphatic "you" address appears, although this time with a positive connotation. Verses 17–22 then draw the consequences from this; like verses 7–12 they are strongly I-centered and threaded with questions. Thus the four parts constitute two parallel pairs:

the actions of YHWH (vv. 2–6, 13–16) and the reaction of the one praying (vv. 7–12, 17–22). In a certain sense the two pairs are even antithetically related: the attention of YHWH described in verses 2–6 is experienced by the one praying as almost like a "siege" (v. 5a), and a burdensome "obligation" (v. 5b) from which she or he wanted to escape and with "one heart" still would like to, even though this is impossible—because of YHWH (vv. 7–12)! The apparently negative and resigned conclusion that closes verses 2–12 is then processed in a positive and combative spirit in verses 13–16, 17–22. In verses 13–16, the one praying attains a deeper insight into God's interest in him or her, by virtue of which she or he has been "set apart" and skillfully fashioned—and which now expects that "God's work" will perform, day by day, the service for which it was created and formed! Even if this duty surpasses the thoughts of the one who prays (vv. 17–18), and this struggle against the wicked and evil itself is properly the responsibility of God alone (v. 19a), he or she will not withdraw from the task, but will address it fully and with all his or her passionate commitment (vv. 21–22).

It should be clear already from this brief sketch that to remove verses 19–22 from the psalm is to destroy the dynamic of the psalm's prayer along with its structure. In this case, the action of the "liturgical reformers" was a deed of artistic and theological barbarity!

But is it still possible to pray verse 19a and verses 21–22 today? If we cannot (and will not) fragment the psalm, must we not remove it from our treasury of prayer? It seems to me that the following observations are useful in answering these questions and aiding us to a deeper understanding of the psalm:

1. Behind verses 17–22 is not an acute threat from enemies, but the very structural violence of "the wicked" (a collective term) who, as "the bloodthirsty," corrupt society and even employ religion for their purposes. In principle, this experience is similar to the one behind Psalm 12, which we considered briefly above.

2. Psalm 139 also shares with Psalm 12 the fundamental conviction that what is at stake in the encounter with the power and success of the violent is the true identity of YHWH-God. But unlike Psalm 12, Psalm 139 is not content merely to protest. The one who prays Psalm 139 feels obligated to concrete resistance and struggle against these enemies of the divine reality. Of course, this is not a struggle motivated by religious fanaticism; it is a battle against "the bloodthirsty," that is, those who criminally destroy human beings.

3. The usage of the First Testament lends the two verbs "hate" and "loathe" different connotations from those they have in modern parlance. "Hate," like "love," refers primarily to concrete action (cf. the love commandment in the First Testament: Lev. 19:17–18, 33–34). In

Psalm 139:21–22 the issue is not an impulse to hatred and loathing of other human beings, but an attitude and actions that oppose and combat destructive violence. On that basis, one could certainly translate these two verses quite accurately and in a way less subject to misunderstanding as follows:

21a   O LORD, should I not combat those who fight against you?
21b   Should I not loathe those who rise up against you?
22a   Indeed, with my whole passion I fight against them:
22b   they have become my enemies.

4. In reality, the one who prays is not forced "by nature" to engage in this struggle against the wicked and against evil. This is clearly and unmistakably stated in verses 7–12. These verses recall Psalm 73, where the one praying confesses, in verses 13–17, that he or she is tempted to go over to the side of the wicked in order to share in their success and riches. Behind Psalm 139:7–12 there appears instead to be an inclination to stand apart from the struggle, or to turn it over to God (cf. also 139:19a). This spontaneous and alarmed withdrawal preserves those who pray it from fanaticism and makes them aware of their dependence on YHWH's support (cf. vv. 23–24!).

5. "Like the one who prays Psalm 73, so also the one who prays this psalm, in contrast to many Sunday churchgoers, cannot ignore the close connection between mystical union with God and politics," writes Othmar Keel. "Injustices in society corrupt our union with God. Much like the 'I' in Psalm 73, the one in Psalm 139 sees how he or she is endangered by this. However, here this awareness and the anxiety it provokes erupt like a volcano into a peaceful landscape."[7] Any kind of trust in God or mysticism that is blind to social injustice or does not want to dirty its hands with such things is, in fact, a form of cynicism.

6. The one who prays is aware of the abiding ambivalence of his or her relationship to God, and struggles with it in prayer. This is the oscillation of dependence, experienced on the one hand as a fundamental limitation and on the other hand as gift. Because of this dependence, Psalm 139 has

for a long time and still today been read as the great poem of the terrible God who watches and controls people, day and night, *from outside,* in order to react with offense, anger, and punishment to a thousand petty details. . . . Psalm 139 is read as the poem of "Big Brother," who exercises a pitiless and total control. But it is not that. Instead, I look to the God who was shaping me while I was still an embryo. Because of that, God knows me better than I know myself. I receive myself as a gift from God and, little by little, learn, in the company of God, to know myself.[8]

In active resistance to injustice and violence, we can become aware of the things that are potentially present in human beings—including an unsuspected strength and creativity.

Psalm 58: A Cry for Right and Justice

1 To the Leader. According to "Do not destroy!" Of (or for) David. A Miktam.
2a Do you indeed decree what is right, you gods?
2b   Do you do justice with rectitude among the children of humanity?
3a No, you deliberately do injustice on the earth,
3b   with your own hands you deal out violence.
4a The wicked go astray from the womb,
4b   those who speak lies err from their mothers' bodies onward.

5a They have venom in them like that of serpents,
5b   like the deaf adder that stops its ear,
6a so that it does not hear the voice of charmers,
6b   or of the cunning enchanter.

7a O God, break the teeth in their mouths,
7b   crush the teeth of the lions, YHWH!

8a Let them vanish like water that runs away,
8b   like grass that is trodden let them wither,
9a like the snail that dissolves into slime,
9b   like the miscarriage of a woman that never sees the sun.
10a Before they can put forth thorns like a briar:
10b   whether green or ablaze, may they be swept away!

11a The righteous will rejoice when they see retribution ("vengeance"),
11b   when they bathe their feet in the blood of the wicked.
12a And people will say, "Surely there is a reward for the righteous,
12b   surely there is a God who does justice on earth!"

This psalm has been excluded from the Liturgy of the Hours. Not only did verses 7 and 11 give offense with their violent and bloodthirsty phrases; but also the imagery of the psalm as a whole, and its vivid descriptions of a desire for destruction, were disturbing to a liturgy that aims at meditative harmony.

The church's tradition was not so squeamish in this regard. Not a few of its teachers and preachers used this psalm to execute verbal destruction on the Jews. Thus, for example, we can read in Augustine's *Enarrationes in Psalmos:*

"God has crushed their teeth in their mouth."
What kind of teeth are these? They are the teeth of those whose

rage is like that of the serpent, of the adder that closes its ears so as not to hear the voice of the charmer. What has the Lord done to them? He has crushed their teeth in their mouth. This has already happened; it happened at the beginning and it is happening now. But would it not be enough, my brethren, if it said, "God has crushed their teeth?" Why "in their mouth"? Like the serpent and the adder, the Pharisees did not wish to hear the law from Christ; they did not desire to hear the words of truth from him. They were content with the sins they had committed, and they did not want to lose their present life; that is, they did not wish to exchange earthly for eternal joys. They closed one ear by their love for what is past, the other by their love for the present: that is why they did not want to hear. And why did they say, "If we let him go on like this, the Romans will come and take away our land and people"? They did not want to lose their land, for they had placed their ear to the ground. It is also written of them that they were greedy and fond of money, and in the gospel the Lord described their whole life, including their past. Whoever reads the gospel with care will find by what means they stopped up both their ears. Understand me, my beloved! What did the Lord do? He crushed their teeth in their mouth. What does this mean, "in their mouth"? They had to testify against themselves out of their own mouth; he compelled them to give judgment against themselves with their own lips. They would have liked to accuse him with the question about taxes, but he did not say that it is permitted to pay taxes, or that it is not permitted. He wanted to crush the teeth with which they tried to bite him, and he wanted to grind them with their own mouths. If he had said, "One ought to pay taxes to Caesar," they would have accused him of degrading the Jewish people by making them subject to taxation. For because of their sins they were so degraded that they had to pay taxes, as prophesied of them in the Law. "We will lay on him," they said, "the degradation of our people, if he commands us to pay taxes; but if he says that we should not pay, we will accuse him of opposing our allegiance to the emperor." They put this dangerous trap before the Lord, in order to catch him. But to whom had they come? To the one who knew how to crush their teeth in their own mouth. "Show me the coin of the tribute," he said. "Why do you test me, you hypocrites? Are you thinking about the payment of taxes? Do you wish to fulfill the obligations of justice? Are you seeking advice on matters of justice? If you are really speaking about justice, then judge rightly, you children of humanity. But because you speak one way and judge another, you are hypocrites. Why do you test me? Now I will shatter your teeth with your own mouth: 'Show me the coin of the tribute!' " And they showed it to him. But he did not say, "This is the emperor's." Instead, he asked, "Whose is it?" Thus he will crush their teeth with their own mouth. For to his question, whose image and inscription these were, they answered, "the emperor's." Now the Lord will crush their teeth with their own mouth. "As soon as you answered, your teeth were crushed with your own mouth. 'Give to the emperor what belongs to the emperor, and to God what belongs to God.' The emperor seeks his image: give it to him. God seeks his image: give it to him. The emperor does not lose his coin, and God does not lose his coin: you are indebted to both of them." But they did not know how to answer. They had been sent to accuse him, and they returned and declared that no one could answer him. Why? Because their teeth were crushed in their mouth. . . . But the Lord has even broken the jaws of the lion. Perhaps it is not unimportant here as well that he does not add "in their mouth." Those who pestered him with trick questions he compelled to declare themselves defeated by their own answers; but those who raged openly were not to be brought down by questions. Nevertheless, their jaws were broken as well: the Crucified One arose and ascended into heaven; Christ was glorified and is adored before all the nations, adored by all kings. Now the Jews may rage if they can. They can no longer: The Lord has broken the jaws of the lions.

(Translated by Linda M. Maloney)

We need not enter into discussion of this allegorizing polemic, but it shows that the spontaneous rejection of Psalm 58 that may occur to some can also be influenced by a "question of taste" that is conditioned by time or situation. Before we surrender to it, we must accept Psalm 58 as a text we can contend with, especially if we can "taste" the layers of expression that are superimposed within it. Then we may even learn to love it!

The two levels of the text can be easily recognized. On the one hand, there is a conflict among the gods, with which the psalm begins (v. 2) and ends (v. 12). We are dealing with the question whether there is a God who protects the order of the world and of living things in such a way that the righteous who live according to that order and act on its behalf are not abandoned. That a righteous life "bears fruit" (is rewarded) is something that "people" should recognize from the fate of the "false gods" and that of "the righteous," in order that they themselves may decide in favor of a life of righteousness.

The second level of the text is visible in verses 4 and 11. Here the opponents in the conflict are not "gods," but the "wicked." On the basis of verse 4, there can be no question but that these are human beings: they are agents of evil "from their mothers' wombs." The gruesome image of war presumed by verse 11 (where "the wicked" is a collective concept) also presumes human beings rather than gods. On this level of the text, the issue is one of a conflict between "the righteous" and "the wicked."

These two different levels of text probably signal two different phases in the origin of the psalm. The basic psalm, which reveals a striking affinity to

Psalm 82, can be sought in verses 2–3, 5–6, 8–10, 12. The scene is a tribunal set up against the "false" gods, who are said to be responsible for the injustice on earth and are therefore threatened with destruction. This original psalm is not a prayer, but a prophetic-didactic poem in the wisdom tradition. The fictional speaker is YHWH, who makes a four-part speech: In verses 2–3 the "gods" are addressed directly in a kind of indictment and trial. The verdict follows in verses 5–6, with the pronouncement of sentence in verses 8–10. Finally, verse 12 formulates the purpose of the destruction of the gods: so that afterward, righteousness may be experienced on earth. In the background of this "basic psalm," whose polemic against the gods points to the world of theological ideas of so-called Deutero-Isaiah, is the idea that the gods control history, and that a true god (or rather, *the* true God) must be judged by whether "there is a reward for the righteous" in that god's realm. Ultimately, this is the question of theodicy. Where the righteous find no justice, God has forfeited existence. That is the provocation embedded in this psalm.

The redaction of the basic psalm found in verses 4, 7, 11 has given a concrete shape to this problem of theodicy. It is meant to deflect the danger that injustice and deeds of violence may be excused or misunderstood as (solely) the work of "gods" or "demons," so that the struggle against evil is seen to be played out merely as a conflict between powers and principalities in the air and in the heavenly realm (cf. Eph. 6:12). In particular, it wishes to see that the struggle over the true God will not cause the sufferings of *human beings* to be forgotten, as well as to avoid the danger that judgment may be postponed until the eschaton. With this in view, the redaction has made the verdict more severe: The failure of the gods is evident from the crimes of the wicked, whose corruption is hyperbolically depicted in verse 4 as a turning aside from the way of righteousness and truth. With the cry for help in verse 7, which has now been artistically fashioned into the structural center of the psalm, the original didactic poem has been transformed into a cry for help coming from those who are terrified to the point of death. That is the situation out of which the psalm must be understood and judged theologically: It is the cry of a person who wishes to live rightly, and for that very reason is in danger of being devoured by a wicked world as if by roaring, wild, voracious lions. This is a cry for rescue uttered by the victims of criminal brutality. Similarly, in verse 11 it is not a question of the satisfaction of fantasies of omnipotence and thirst for vengeance, but of the accomplishment and restoration of right and justice. Certainly, the image of the righteous wading in the blood of the slain criminals is an image of terror that alarms and repels us, and because of the emotional potential for aggression that it can arouse in us it is highly problematic. It is possible to discuss whether and how we can formulate this extreme metaphor in words that make its legal background clearer (cf. chapter 4 below). But in any case we must take note of three points if we are to do justice to this psalm, or this verse of the psalm.

1. Those who pray this psalm subject themselves to the maxim for life that verse 12 proclaims to be the quintessence of the psalm: only the righteous will be rewarded. And the true God decides who the righteous are.
2. This psalm, and especially verse 11, is not concerned with irrational "vengeance," but with "retribution" (translating here with Martin Buber)—that is, the rescue of the victims of injustice, and the public restoration of the right order that had been destroyed, for the good of humanity (cf. v. 12).
3. The psalm fights for the indispensable union of religion and ethics. The truth about God that people believe or proclaim can be tested by whether it preserves its adherents from the ways of violence and impels them to a life in solidarity with the victims of violence.

Psalm 83: Witness for God, When Everything Else Is a Denial of God

1   A Song. A Psalm of/for Asaph.
2a   Elohim, do not keep silence,
2b   do not hold your peace or be still, El!
3a   For see, your enemies are in tumult
3b   and those who hate you have raised their heads.
4a   They lay crafty plans against your people
4b   and consult together against those you protect.
5a   They say, "Come, let us wipe them out as a nation
5b   and never more shall the name of Israel be remembered!"
6a   Indeed, they conspire together with one accord,
6b   against you they make a covenant:
7a   the tents of Edom and the Ishmaelites,
7b   Moab and the Hagrites,
8a   Gebal and Ammon and Amalek,
8b   Philistia with the inhabitants of Tyre,
9a   Assyria also has joined them,
9b   they are the strong arm of the children of Lot. *Selah.*

10a Do to them as you did to Midian,
10b   as to Sisera and Jabin at the Wadi Kishon,
11a who were destroyed at En-dor,
11b   who became dung for the ground,
12a make their nobles like Oreb and Zeeb,

12b	all their princes like Zebah and Zalmunna,
13a	who said, "Let us take as our own possession
13b	the pastures of Elohim."
14a	My Elohim, make them like a tumbleweed,
14b	like chaff before the wind.
15a	As fire consumes the forest,
15b	as the flame sets the mountains ablaze,
16a	so pursue them with your tempest
16b	and terrify them with your hurricane.
17a	Fill their faces with shame,
17b	so that they may seek your name, YHWH.
18a	Let them be put to shame and dismayed forever,
18b	let them perish in disgrace.
19a	Let them know that you alone, whose name is YHWH,
19b	are the Most High (Elyon) over all the earth.

It is not surprising that Psalm 83 also fell victim to official church censorship for the Liturgy of the Hours, if we note the "scholarly" qualifications and reservations directed at it in one group of critical commentaries on the psalms, even though, in comparison to the other two incriminated "psalms of cursing," 58 and 109, Psalm 83 comes off relatively well.

On the one hand, there are some remarks that even expressly recommend that the church use Psalm 83 in particular situations—not, however, as a "witness for God," but as a "prayer in struggle and petition for endurance." Thus, for example, Heinz Reinelt gives the following advice in the series "Geistliche Schriftlesung" [Spiritual Reading of Scripture]:

> The Christian who prays this psalm must translate the threat to the people of God so compactly described here by the Old Testament psalmist into an image of the combined attacks to which the church has been exposed in the course of its history, and to which it will continue to be exposed, corresponding to the fate of our Lord Jesus Christ. One can pray this psalm in the light of its concluding statement.[9]

An analogous perspective is also suggested by Alfons Deissler, who understands the enemies of the church combatted in the psalm in a much broader sense:

> While in the Old Testament context our psalm is fully legitimate, on the level of the new covenant the horizon of its understanding must of course be expanded. The names of the enemies listed here become symbols for all the powers opposed to God, among and behind which sin, death, and Satan are at work (cf. Rev. 13 and 20:7–10). The pleas of the Christian who prays this psalm implore that they be again and again divested of their power. The petition in verse 17—which should not be ignored!—will thus receive the

strongest accent. For Christians in particular, the ultimate and highest desire must be that all people "seek God's name."[10]

We may also locate the position of Otto Spülbeck, the bishop of Meißen, (which was formerly part of East Germany), within the horizon of this prayer perspective. In 1965, as a member of the committee which discussed the retention or elimination of the "psalms of cursing" in the Liturgy of the Hours, he said:

> Our special [i. e., political] circumstances require that the entire Psalter be used. Afflicted as we are by a very difficult external situation, we need expressions suitable for use *contra diabolum*.[11]

This position probably also underlies the decision to provide for the use of Psalm 83:19, 14 in the renewed liturgy of the Mass as a responsorial psalm "for Christians who are persecuted for their faith," after the reading of Acts 4:23–31. This selection and rearrangement of the text is not only highly problematic in itself (for example, how can one do without the opening lament in verse 2 of the psalm?). The reversal of the sequence of verses also shows that the theological dynamic of the psalm (see below) has not been understood, or rather, that it has been misunderstood in a typically Christian fashion.

The "positive" Christian attempts at appropriation of Psalm 83 have in common that they deprive it of its concrete reference to Israel, and create an allegorizing reference to the church. In contrast, where commentators give more concentrated attention to the theology of history developed in Psalm 83:10–16, one senses their uneasiness and lack of understanding. Both attitudes are succinctly summarized in the commentary on the Psalms in *The Interpreter's Bible* (1955):

> This psalm is an unedifying and tedious catalogue of bloody violence. . . . These factors are largely responsible for the consensus that regards this psalm as one of the least religious of all the poems in the Psalter. It is so completely given over to irritation and vindictiveness that however much credit we may assign to the pious hope with which it ends, it is all but wholly lacking in any of the overtones of devotion, trust, and godly sorrow that redeem the other imprecatory psalms.[12]

Even a limited glance at the prayer-dynamic of this psalm, however, can make it clear that Psalm 83, whose concluding clause has become part of the Gloria in the Mass, contains—in my opinion—an indispensable theological message.

This postexilic psalm is (whether explicitly or implicitly) constituted throughout as an appellative address to God in the second person singular;

the opening three vetitives in verse 2 and the four imperatives in verses 10, 12, 14, and 17 impart a positively combative and demanding urgency to this "you" address. This is a struggle with God to extract proof that God is indeed God in and for Israel—a proof to be established in the forum of the nations of the world. Israel here makes itself the attorney on behalf of the cause of God; it does so on the basis of its experience that YHWH and Israel belong together like two sides of a single coin. When Israel is threatened, YHWH, as God of Israel, is also threatened. If Israel's name vanishes, YHWH, the God of Israel, will also "vanish." To exaggerate: In this psalm, Israel screams at YHWH to do something, finally, to ensure YHWH's own "survival." This dramatic point is given strong and emphatic expression in the opening and closing lines of the psalm. While both cola of verse 2 are shaped in such a way that they are framed by the divine titles *Elohim* and *El,* the two cola in verse 19 bring the divine names or titles YHWH and *El* together in the middle. It is only in these two parallelisms that the express naming of God occurs in each of these lines, while the process of divine proof that is at issue is very artistically summarized: As a silent God, the divine being is called *Elohim* or *El,* and is in some sense a distant God, a divinity without name or face; this God, we might say, has disappeared into the crowd of gods acknowledged by the nations. Still worse, these nations are already busy at the task of eliminating, even destroying, God. Therefore Israel appeals urgently to God in this psalm, using extreme images of its dread and recollections of its constitutive history with God, to beg that God will finally desist from being distant and weary, and will stand forth, self-revealed in "your name," YHWH, which simultaneously describes God's particular and universal divinity (v. 19). All the statements in the psalm are subordinated to this cry of Israel, imploring that YHWH will awaken from this dangerous self-forgetfulness; this is true also of the so-called appeals for cursing and destruction. The passion of this psalm is Israel's own suffering with its God; it is a painful sense of the absence of God in light of the ambivalent historical experiences in the collective memory of Israel that the psalm recalls and conjures up.

The psalm is clearly divided into two parts, as the *Selah* at the end of verse 9 indicates. The first part (vv. 2–9) is an appeal and protest against a God who, untouched, unmoved, or even powerlessly accepts the thrusts of the nations against God's people and God's own self. The appeal begins with the threefold, intensifying vetitive series in which the whole of Israel's "God-darkness" is concentrated: That YHWH speaks, acts, permits access; in short, that YHWH is a living God, dwelling in and with YHWH's people—all this is the core affirmation of the traditional faith of Israel, and that faith itself would and will be proven untrue and irrelevant by Israel's history, as it is graphically developed in the recital of evidence in verses 3–9. This complex of evidence, in turn, consists of two sections: verses 3–6 and 7–9.

The first section, verses 3–6, is a chiastic composition lamenting the plans of the enemy nations directed against YHWH and YHWH's people (v. 3: against YHWH; vv. 4–5: against YHWH's people; v. 6: against YHWH). The hostile actions are described, on the one hand, with personalized metaphors: the enemies "hate," they "raise their heads," they "lay crafty plans" among themselves, they have a "heart" and an "arm." Correspondingly, even the transcendent YHWH is described as so immanent and concrete as to appear threatened and endangered as a person: "against you they make a covenant" (v. 6b). On the other hand, the first verb, "to be in tumult," which comes from the vocabulary of the struggle against chaos, gives a mythic dimension to the entire action; it is in this dimension that the elementary and fundamental meaning of the conflict here described is expressed.

It is clear, both from the conspiratorial words laid in the mouths of the nations in verse 5 and from the formulation "they make a covenant" in verse 6b, which summarizes the situation depicted, that what is at issue is not a special attack on Israel, but the mythical attack of the nations against YHWH and YHWH's divine existence, which is bound up with Israel. The "covenant" thus made is chosen as a deliberate opposition to the YHWH-Israel relationship, also conceived as a "covenant." Even in this short section of the psalm, the special role of Israel as witness to God is evident: Because Israel believes in a God who acts within history, it must draw that God so deeply into history, both in the way it speaks of God and in its metaphorical depictions, that God's figurative shape becomes elemental and concrete to the point that it can no longer be separated from history. That is the unique demand of the Jewish-Christian message about God, and it is intensified in the "prayers for cursing and destruction" in this psalm to the point that it appears almost insupportable. For Christians, who have concentrated the immanent aspect of divine action in the life and death of Jesus, a relatively modest event in the light of history, such a complex and concrete "incarnation" of God in the history of Israel is understandably a challenge,[13] as shown by the discussion of the "cursing psalms" sketched above.

The radicality with which our psalm senses and interprets the calling into question of YHWH's divine identity by history can also be observed in the artistically shaped tableau of the enemy nations, which now follows as a second section (vv. 7–9) in which the actors in the plotting lamented in verses 3–6 are named. Against the repeated attempts among exegetes to interpret this section in terms of a unique historical constellation, we must insist that the poetic-symbolic configuration of the section alone indicates that what is at issue is the catastrophic side of Israel's history as a whole. The names of the nations and tribes are emblems for the world's peoples who surrounded Israel and who were experienced by it in the course of its history as enemies to be feared. From a formal point of view this "tableau of the nations" reveals five characteristics that are relevant for the interpretation: First, ten nations are listed, thus making clear already that they represent a totality, a kind of historical summary. Second, the series of ten is divided, from a linguistic and stylistic point of view, into sets of nine and one. Verses 7–8 offer a list of nine names; then, in verse 9, Assyria appears, syntactically set apart, as a tenth member. Thus this historical summary points to two levels of history: here are the minor agents who are, in turn, supported and driven by a major actor. Third, the arrangement of the nine minor nations follows a geographical pattern that evokes the threatening encirclement of Israel from east and west. Fourth, the selection of names is apparently a reference to the traditions that relate Israel's route to the Promised Land and the settlement of the land itself. Fifth, the fact that precisely nine names are grouped together is probably connected to the idea of the "nine-ness" of the nations, repeatedly attested in Egyptian iconography and national theology, as well as to the "nine bows" symbolizing all the nations subjected to the Egyptian king. Thus when our psalm laments the revolt of this group of nine enemy nations, Israel is summoning the idea of YHWH's role as the one who binds chaos to create cosmos.

The second section (vv. 10–19), in three separate initiatives, demands that YHWH act; throughout the three, the intensity of the plea for the divine self-demonstration increases, both in the imagery and in the use of names and titles for God. Verses 10–13, alluding to Judges 4–8, recall the "primeval" action of YHWH against Israel's enemies, although an explicit reference to God is found only in the speech of the enemies, presented as a quotation; the images that are employed make concrete not the action of YHWH, but the fate of the enemies. In contrast, the next part (vv. 14–16) begins emphatically with an address to God as "my Elohim" and uses images from the vocabulary of nature-theophanies; the enclitic personal suffixes of the second person singular in verse 16 prepare for the personal aspect of the coming of God, which we then encounter in the final part, verses 17–19, with the double invocation of the name of YHWH to drive home the point. The images in this last part, which take up the conventionalized language of the psalms, sketch the confrontation between YHWH and the enemy nations as a personal encounter that will lead to the acknowledgment of YHWH by the nations and thus to an end of the history of Israel's suffering that is lamented in the psalm. This very intensification of the metaphorical language and of YHWH's means of revelation must be taken into account if the "prayers for destruction" in the psalm are to be rightly understood.

These are images *for* God, that is, metaphors that put pressure on YHWH by recalling YHWH's own constitutive history with Israel and at the same time, as metaphors, leave to YHWH's discretion the fulfillment of these images. It is precisely the central absurdity of the biblical metaphors for God, misunderstood as something insupportable, that is meant to cause a "semantic shock"[14] that leads to a new knowledge of God. What we are asked to do is to expose ourselves to the incompatibility and insupportability of the biblical metaphors for God, so that we will not miss or destroy the complex reality of God by freezing it in particular concepts. The metaphors for God, with their power of utterance that surpasses the familiar and the obvious, make possible, and even demand, a history of new and surprising discoveries about God, because history itself repeatedly calls into question these assertions about God, and at the same time offers new realizations and ways of understanding. The fascination and vitality of the history of Israel's faith "results decisively from the fact . . . that they did not retreat from the semantic insupportability of the central God-metaphors into a rapid comprehension of superficial correspondences, and did not surrender the will to understand when the superficial correspondences collapsed."[15]

Israel's passionate adherence to the truth about God as a search for new experiences of God is expressed primarily in the montage of God-metaphors that serve, in combination, only to intensify the "semantic shock," as in verses 10–13, 14–16, 17–19. The drama becomes more powerful here because the metaphorical speech is shaped as a prayer, or an appeal to God. Thus the combined God-metaphors in verses 10–19 are images of God in a twofold sense: On the one hand, they name the experiences of God in the collective consciousness and attempt to understand the truth of them anew, precisely in light of their being called into question by history. In them, in a sense, Israel assumes the task of reshaping and relearning what had heretofore been metaphorically associated with YHWH and YHWH's coming to create justice.

On the other hand, these are images that are held up in appeal to YHWH, in order that YHWH may exhaust anew the divine potential they invoke—for the sake of YHWH's own truth. For that reason, the tensions and contradictions between individual elements in the montage of metaphors in verses 10–19 may not be dissolved through literary-critical analysis, nor theologically simplified into a single statement. Above all, the third section must not be misunderstood as an orthodox softening. It urges YHWH, as God of Israel, now finally to be revealed as Elyon, that is, the one from Zion who battles chaos—corresponding to the name YHWH, the one whose protective and saving power the psalm invokes with its metaphoric evocation of YHWH as the war-god of Israel's beginnings. The metaphoric allusion to the narratives of the rescue of Israel from the Canaanites and the Midianites, who wanted to take from Israel the land given by God, does not urge a naive repetition of these wars (which would deprive YHWH of the historical dimension and turn the God of Israel into a mythical divine figure!). Rather, the metaphoric field with which this psalm works is a combination of epiphany

(vv. 10–16) and theophany (vv. 17–19) that is to lead to an acknowledgment of YHWH on the part of *all* the nations—and thus to the rescue of Israel. From the point of view of this goal, the psalm is a realization of Israel's witness to God, which changes Israel itself and will work toward the changing of the nations as well—in a situation in which the traditional language about YHWH as the saving and protecting God, the universal guarantor of right and justice, appears to be refuted by the realities of history. Israel's powerful-powerless cry to and for God is both the reality *that,* and the way in *which* it expresses its testimony to God in the face of this painful situation. It is a cry that gives the strength to hope that YHWH will prove, in and through Israel, to be God in this world. In this, Israel's testimony to God, surrendering everything to its God YHWH in the most extreme situation of doubt about God, God's justice is attested as love for those who are oppressed and persecuted.

There should be a more lengthy development of the dimensions that echo in the content of the eighty-third psalm's testimony to God, and what that means for the question of Christian reception of the psalm. For our particular questions, and for the theological "evaluation" of the psalm, the following points are important:

1. At the beginning and at the end, in a kind of frame, the psalm alludes to the final verse of the Song of Deborah (Judg. 5:31), and verse 10 makes it clear that the psalm as a whole takes up the traditions in Judges 4–5 and makes them metaphorically present. The correlation with Judges 5 lends the psalm a number of connotations: The vetitives that open the psalm are thus to be heard as a cry to the saving God who comes from Sinai, to whose epiphany the related motifs in Judges 5:4–5, 20 and Psalm 83:14–16 also point. On the other hand, the comparison with Judges 5 sets in sharp relief the altered theological profile of Psalm 83, to the extent that verse 19 is to be read as an express continuation of the conclusion of Judges 5: The revelation of the God of Sinai is certainly aimed at the salvation of Israel as the people of God (cf. Ps. 83:4–5 with Judg. 5:11, 13), but at the same time, and still more, at the transformation of the enemy nations. The contrast between verses 3 and 19, which is also highlighted by the compositional structure of the psalm, indicates that this psalm no longer hopes for the end of the enemies of God, but rather for an end to enmity toward God. The *attack of the nations* against YHWH and YHWH's people (vv. 2–4) is transformed by YHWH's intervention, and becomes a *pilgrimage of the nations* (vv. 17b) and *homage of the nations* (v. 19). All the other awkward individual statements in this psalm are to be interpreted in reference to this fundamental dynamic.

2. Psalm 83 is not only related in many ways to Psalms 46–48 on the basis of motifs. Especially in the structure of events, it is so strongly oriented to Psalm 46 that it should be read as a complaint entered against the vision of the inbreaking of the universal reign of YHWH's peace that is presented in that confident psalm.[16]

3. The structure of events in Psalm 83, as is usually pointed out in the commentaries as well, corresponds to that of Psalm 2, which contains a similarly contrasting and tension-filled montage of metaphors; there are even a number of key words that are common to these two psalms.[17] Whether and how the relationship between the two is to be explained in terms of dependency of one on the other is something that cannot be discussed here. However, it is important for the theological understanding of Psalm 83 that Psalm 2 also applies its metaphors of violence in order to bring Israel and the nations together under the divine rule of YHWH.

4. In the background of Psalm 83 is also the vision presented hymnically in Psalm 100 as the conclusion to the series of "YHWH is king" Psalms 93–99, in which Israel and the nations are joined together in a common witness to God as the God of Sinai. Psalm 100 can even be read as a continuation and exegesis of Psalm 83:17–19.

5. The appeal that, as one among others, opens Psalm 83, "do not keep silence!" is a backward reference, within a canonical reading, to the first psalm of Asaph, at 50:3: "Our God comes and does not keep silence." The theophany of YHWH announced in Psalm 50, in which YHWH proclaims divine law to the people, setting it up for judgment in the midst of the people and bringing it to effect, not only there but on the universal stage (Ps. 50:2), is made concrete in the Asaph Psalm 83 as an event that is communicated to all the nations that live upon that stage. The line of tension between Psalms 50 and 83 then at the same time interprets the meaning of the acknowledgment of YHWH by the nations that is demanded in Psalm 83:17, 19: It is to be an acceptance of the law of God revealed at Sinai and going forth from Zion.

6. The multiple key words common to Psalms 83 and 73 emphasize that Psalm 83 is not to be misunderstood as the expression of a nationalistic or triumphalistic lust for power. These related words are a palpable witness both to Israel's suffering with and because of its God, and at the same time, to its vivid longing for God.

7. When read as the last of the twelve (!) Asaph psalms (Pss. 50, 73–83), Psalm 83 reveals itself in a very poignant sense as a "theodicy psalm." This does not, of course, mean that God is "justified," but that here God's righteousness is invoked in such a way that it cries

out against YHWH's very self the wrong that threatens YHWH's own divinity—and carries out this cry against YHWH as a metaphor of hope by its confidence that YHWH will, in fact, not accept and permit this wrong.

Psalm 137: What Remains for the Powerless

1a By the streams of Babylon—
1b   there we sat down and wept
1c   when we remembered Zion.
2a On the poplars there
2b   we hung up our harps.
3a For there our captors asked us for songs,
3b   and our tormentors asked for mirth, saying,
3c   "Sing us one of the songs of Zion!"
4a How could we sing a song of YHWH
4b   in a foreign land?
5a If I forget you, O Jerusalem,
5b   let my right hand forget itself,
6a Let my tongue cling to the roof of my mouth,
6b   if I do not remember you,
6c if I do not set Jerusalem
6d   above my highest joy.

7a Remember, YHWH, against the Edomites
7b   the day of Jerusalem.
7c They said, "Tear it down! Tear it down!
7d   Down to its foundations!"
8a O daughter Babylon, you devastator:
8b   Happy shall they be who pay you back
8c   what you have done to us!
9a Happy shall they be who take your children
9b   and smash them against the stones!

Psalm 137, written in exile, is regarded as the "psalm of violence" par excellence, and, at least in its full text, to be rejected by Christians (even though its beginning has been incorporated in the treasury of Christian quotations, and a few years ago, in the musical setting by the group Boney M, was one of the catchiest items in the repertoire of young people's discotheque music). Even Alfons Deissler concludes his generally sensitive interpretation of this psalm by saying:

> Psalm 137 is one of the most gripping and poetically one of the best songs in the psalter. If we put ourselves entirely in the situation of

> those who prayed it at the time, our hearts follow, and suddenly
> even the scandalous final verse is understandable within the hori-
> zon of the psychology of the time. But a Christian may never sur-
> render to this mentality. In Luke 9:54–55, Jesus draws a line that is
> never to be crossed: The disciples are not permitted to call down
> fire from heaven on their opponents. Jesus' words and example
> (Matt. 5:44; Luke 23:34; cf. Rom. 12:19–20) teach, beyond any pos-
> sibility of other interpretation, that we should pray for our perse-
> cutors, and not curse them. Therefore the concluding verse (8) of
> Psalm 137 should be removed from the psalter of the new people
> of God. Even Revelation 18:2–8 does not justify it as a prayer of the
> church on earth.[18]

Of course, the elimination of verses 8–9 would not only destroy the literary
structure of the psalm, but would deprive it of an essential key to a correct
and theologically acceptable (!) understanding of its perspective on violence. Verses 8–9 are not, as a hasty erasure of them alleges, a "blessing" on
child-murderers; they are a passionate outcry of the powerless demanding
justice!

Psalm 137 is not the song of people who have the power to effect a violent change in their situation of suffering, nor is it the battle cry of terrorists. Instead, it is an attempt to cling to one's historical identity even when
everything is against it. Still more, it is an attempt, in the face of the most
profound humiliation and helplessness, to suppress the primitive human
lust for violence in one's own heart, by surrendering *everything* to God—a
God whose word of judgment is presumed to be so universally just that even
those who pray the psalm submit themselves to it.

The psalm divides into two parts: in verses 1–6, those who pray lament
their own internal conflict, into which they have been cast by their situation
in the strange land of Babylon. In a single freeze-frame, the structural violence and mockery of their "captors" as well as the whole spectrum of their
contradictory situation is captured. Their "tormentors" mock them with the
"songs of Zion" in which they used to sing of YHWH as the protector of
Mount Zion and those who live on it (cf. Pss. 46 and 48). Their Babylonian
exile and the destruction of Jerusalem ("the day of Jerusalem," cf. v. 7) is,
in the eyes of the Babylonians, the clear proof of the falsehood of YHWH's
intimate relationship to Zion that was praised in those songs. To sing "songs
of Zion" in this situation would be pure derision. What is appropriate now,
in fact, is doubt about God. And yet they cling to YHWH and YHWH's promises
to Zion. What else can they hold to? Of course, they have to produce this
constancy out of themselves, and with difficulty, as verses 5–6 show. Against
the power of reality and their own powerlessness they oppose the oath-tak-
ing gesture that proclaims a hope of receiving *everything* from YHWH, to

whom they surrender themselves completely. This is the meaning of verses 5–6: "In taking an oath, the one swearing must make the symbolic gesture of holding his or her throat with one hand while speaking the words. Should the psalmist forget Jerusalem in that instant of swearing, the hand will forget the one who swears, and will constrict the throat. The result will be that the person will suffocate, expressed in the psalm through the realistic description of a person in the throes of suffocation, whose tongue sticks to the roof of the mouth."[19]

After lifting up their unconditional adherence to YHWH and Jerusalem, those who pray the psalm then in the second part, which is clearly separated from the first by its language, appeal to YHWH in turn to demonstrate adherence to YHWH's people and city, Jerusalem, as a historical reality—by means of the public restoration of the order of justice that has been despised and destroyed by Edom and Babylon (vv. 7–9).

The following points are important for our reflection:

1. The theocentricity of the psalm is constitutive for the whole of it(!). The theme of the complaint is not the external distress of the deported, but their fear that YHWH has abandoned YHWH's relationship to Zion—or even the fear that the divine reality of YHWH that had been revealed from Zion (Jerusalem) had been proved by the power of the Babylonians to be lying and deceit. Therefore the theme of the cry for help and the blessings in the second part is not the future of Israel, but the historical experience that neither Edom's fraternal betrayal nor the brutality of Babylon can be the last word. Thus this psalm is part of the group of "theodicy psalms." Of course, it is not a question of a justification of God after the fact, but of a complaint that the status quo contradicts the truth about God that had been believed and hoped for—and that this status quo is therefore unacceptable. Those, including the "liturgical reformers," who will only permit verses 1–6 to be prayed or sung as a defensibly "Christian" psalm rob it of its theocentric dynamic, which is essentially connected to the appeal to God in verses 7–9. Only through verse 7, in fact, does the psalm become, in its language and literary form, a *prayer to God!*

2. The whole psalm is shaped by legal categories and ideas of right and justice. Contrary to first impressions, it is based on neither feelings of hatred nor irrational vengeance. The very first part of the psalm, with its gesture of swearing formulated in terms of the *lex talionis* (the law of retaliation), evokes the fundamental order of justice established and protected by YHWH, to which those praying also submit themselves. This is still more the case with the especially difficult verses 8–9.

Here the form itself—the beatitude, from the wisdom tradition—evokes the idea of retributive justice (the so-called relationship of action and consequence), which is the foundation not only of individual social relationships, but primarily that of nations. The issue in verses 8–9 is the public restoration of the world order. When, at the present time, the sanctions of international law are demanded and imposed against aggressors and political terrorists, such action has as little to do with "revenge" as does the appeal in verses 8–9 to a power that will put Babylon in its place.

3. The psalm is a poetic and emotional expression of doubt about God and of the vivid anxieties of the deported. It exists fully *from* and *in* its imagery, which must be understood *as such*, and not, in fact, as political strategy. Precisely the image in verse 9, which for us is so shocking and repellent at first glance, expresses first of all Israel's experience of powerlessness (!), something lived in its full reality by these people in their confrontation with the Babylonian war machine and the ideology of world dominance that stood behind it. This immense power for violence is opposed, in Psalm 137:8–9, by the hope that there will be a reversal of power—but *only in order that* this superfluous power for violence will be ended once and for all. It is extraordinarily important to realize that this psalm does *not* pray that Israel and Babylon should simply exchange roles (as, for example, in the Magnificat: cf. Luke 1:52). Instead, remaining entirely within the theocentricity of the psalm, the issue is a demonstration of justice in the very face of a power that pretends that the violent force it exercises to oppress the nations is, in fact, right.

4. Psalm 137 is a political psalm: It deals with the end of Babylon's reign of terror. This is also important with respect to the image of the children of daughter Babylon, who are to be smashed against the stone pavements of the capital city. "The children" are those of the royal house, that is, of the dynasty (cf. Isa. 7:14–16; 9:1–6). The horrible image means to say that this dynasty of terror ought to be exterminated completely ("root and branch"). In the last chapter we will present some thoughts on the question of an alternative translation of Psalm 137:9. (See chapter 4 below.)

5. The appeal to the God who protects a just world order is rooted, for those who pray Psalm 137, in the recollection of the love of YHWH for Zion/Jerusalem/Israel experienced in history. Therefore the passionate language of the psalm is the expression of passionate love—and can be properly understood and comprehended only by those who love. Those who confuse the longing of love with a plan of action will never understand Psalm 137.

Psalm 44: Transformation of the Image
of a Violent God

There are, in the book of Psalms, a number of psalms in and through which Israel surrenders itself so intensively to the problem of an all too violent image of God that, in the process, that image literally collapses and is transformed into something new. According to traditional exegetical methods, this process can on the one hand be traced diachronically, as a successive historical learning process occasioned by catastrophic experiences in which Israel itself became the victim of violence. On the other hand, one may also read these psalms synchronically in such a way that one finds reflected in them the enduring complexity of language about God, to the extent that a God of love without power would only be a powerless God who would be forced to surrender the powerless to the violence of the cruel—and thus could "motivate" people only to resignation.

The paradigm of such a metamorphosis of the divine image is the popular song of lament that forms Psalm 44. Diachronically speaking, we can recognize in it two levels of text in which we can follow the learning process to which Israel exposed itself as, in the catastrophic experiences of the destruction of Jerusalem, the loss of independent political power, submission to foreign powers, internal conflicts, and profound doubt about God, it found the strength to cling to its God, YHWH, who appeared powerless because apparently defeated by the gods of Babylon, and to hope in YHWH's loving relationship to Israel.

The basic level of Psalm 44 (vv. 2–9)* stems from the preexilic period and relies totally on the God who has in the past produced proof of being a God of war and victory, and who is now to prove it once again.

The psalm begins with the recollection of the origins of the relationship between YHWH and Israel:

2a   We have heard with our ears, O God,
2b   our ancestors have told us
2c   a deed you performed in their days,
2d/3a   in the days of the first beginning; you with your own hand
3b   destroyed the nations, but them you planted;
3c   you afflicted the peoples, but them you set free;
4a   for not by their own sword did they win the land,
4b   nor did their own arm give them rescue;
4c   but your right hand, and your arm,
4d   and the light of your countenance, for you delighted in them.

Translator's note: Again the author's numbering takes the first line, "To the leader. Of the Korahites. A Maskil," as verse 1, and all subsequent verse numbers are advanced one number from those given in English editions.

Here we find sketched a frighteningly vigorous image of the beginnings of Israel in Canaan. The God of Israel personally cut down the land like a forest, in order to install Israel as a new planting and give it the power to grow mightily (cf. also Ps. 80:9–12). This anamnesis is the basis of the petition that follows:

> 5a   You are my King, O God;
> 5b   command victories for Jacob!
> 6a   With you we press down our foes;
> 6b   through your name we tread down our assailants.
> 7a   For not in my bow do I trust,
> 7b   nor can my sword save me.
> 8a   But you have saved us from our foes,
> 8b   and have put to confusion those who hate us.

With the help and through the strength of this Super-God, those who pray the psalm wish to be like a steer throwing down with its horns the enemies besetting them, and trampling them under foot (cf. Deut. 33:17; 1 Kgs. 22:11; Ezek. 34:21; and especially Ps. 60:14). And in a concluding vow of praise they remind their God of how much God's very divine existence depends on the fulfillment of this plea:

> 9a   We have always boasted that you are our God,
> 9b   and we intend to praise your name to the end of time.

As we know, history did not see the realization of this appeal which Israel addressed to its God at the end of the 7th century B.C.E. Even the great reforming king Josiah was slain by the hand of the Egyptians as he fought to defend the land (cf. 2 Kgs. 23:29). But even more, what Israel wished to do to its enemies fell upon Israel itself in the catastrophe of 587 B.C.E., and threw it into a deep identity crisis, as well as a crisis over God, in the course of which there grew up an awareness that the history of the God YHWH with this people is apparently not the constant achievement of deeds of power, and the definition of this God's divinity does not consist in the destruction of "the nations." That, at least, is the insight achieved by the exiled groups who expanded the preexilic basis of Psalm 44 and shaped it into a new psalm. The theological breakthrough succeeded for them because, on the one hand, it confronted the reality of the catastrophe, and on the other hand, it proposed to withstand it precisely by holding fast to the God who had become incomprehensible to them.

They drew a sober conclusion. In spite of the praise given to the divine power, they had found:

> 10a   Yet you have rejected us and abased us!
> 10b   You have [apparently] not gone to war with our armies.

That is the truth that, a century and a half earlier, the prophet Isaiah had incessantly but fruitlessly preached: YHWH is not a war god, and staking everything on power is idolatry. Now Israel had to learn this truth through a painful process:

11a You made us turn back from the foe,
11b   and our enemies have gotten spoil [from us].
12a You have made us like sheep for slaughter,
12b   and have scattered us among the nations.
13a You have sold your people for a trifle,
13b   demanding no high price for them.
14a You have made us the taunt of our neighbors,
14b   the derision and scorn of those around us.
15a You have made us a byword among the nations,
15b   a laughingstock [a shaking of the head, literally] among the
         peoples.
16a All day long my disgrace is before me,
16b   and shame has covered my face
17a at the words of the taunters and revilers,
17b   at the sight of the enemy and the avenger.

The text formulates with extraordinary acerbity: You, our God, have done this, and you are still doing it! Verse 13 sums up the whole contradictory situation: God has one single people, and that people God has dumped at sale prices, without even taking the trouble to try to make a profit on this "transaction." Is God's people really worth no more to God than that? Is God not worth more? What kind of a shepherd would take so much care in raising a flock, and then expose them everywhere to be torn by human beings and wild beasts (cf. Pss. 23:1; 80:2)?

But those who pray this psalm do not remain mired in complaint and accusation. In a further section (vv. 18–23) they seek for a deeper reason for their distress. They do not take over the deuteronomistic theology of sin and punishment. Their eyes are not turned simply to the past. For them, instead, the catastrophe is a current challenge that they intend to face:

18a All this has come upon us, yet we have not forgotten you,
18b   or been false to your covenant.
19a Our heart has not turned back,
19b   nor have our steps departed from your way,
20a even when you have broken us in the haunt of jackals,
20b   and covered us with deep darkness.

They want to hold to their God with all their minds (v. 19a) and actions (v. 19b), even in this situation in which they are literally desert-ed (v. 20a: "the haunt of jackals") and in the darkness of God, a darkness God has personally spread over them (v. 20b). And so they arrive at one of the most pro-

found, and at the same time most painful statements about the existence of
Israel:

21a   If we had forgotten the name of our God,
21b   or spread out our hands to a strange god,
22a   would not God discover this?
22b   for God knows the secrets of the heart.
23a   Because of you we are being killed all day long,
23b   and accounted as sheep for the slaughter.

Because Israel sought its national identity, with an utterly prophetic passion, in its covenant with God, it has become a beast for slaughter (cf. similarly Ps. 69:8; Jer. 15:15; Isa. 53:7). Because Israel was chosen by YHWH as
YHWH's *own* people, in which YHWH's divinity is to be revealed, it must suffer. It must experience in the flesh that YHWH is not on the side of the powerful and the victors, but on the side of the weak and suffering. As this psalm
sees it, it is in its decision to withstand its suffering and thereby not to forget YHWH—in suffering *because of* its God—that Israel can and will be
witness to this new divine reality, in contrast to the preexilic psalm. Of
course, it is precisely in this situation that the people of God need confidence that their suffering is not estrangement from God, but a special close-
ness to God. That is why the psalm concludes with an outcry and a complaint of enormous intensity, appealing to God to look at it and accept it:

24a   Rouse yourself! Why do you sleep, O Lord?
24b   Awake, do not cast us off forever!
25a   Why do you hide your face?
25b   Why do you forget our affliction and oppression?
26a   For our soul sinks down to the dust;
26b   our body clings to the ground.
27a   Rise up, come to our help,
27b   and redeem us for the sake of your steadfast love!

With an allusion to the exodus as redemption from foreign enslavement
and the danger of death, the psalm prays for an end to the alienation between YHWH and YHWH's people. It is an outcry that no longer seeks the all-
powerful God, but rather the all-merciful God. It is a cry arising from a passionate "why?" and "wherefore?" to seek an approach to God, the God who
is present and abiding in the night of futility and suffering. This cry em-
anates from that original union rooted in Israel's origins and reaffirmed
here again—although this time as complaint and plea: YHWH is implored to
prove again to be the God of Exodus who knows their suffering and suffers
with them. The impetuous question: "Why do you hide your face?" is one
of those real, life-and-death questions, because it arises from an indissolu-
ble relationship of those who suffer to the God of Israel, and surrenders to
the promise so profoundly expressed in Exodus 3:14: "I am present [with

you], and I will be present [with you]"—even though differently from the
way in which the gods of the nations are present, and differently from the
way in which you, Israel, often and repeatedly wish that I were!

Psalm 109: They Attack Me without Cause,
but I Am a Prayer

1a   To the leader. A Psalm of David.
1b   Do not be silent, O God of my praise!
2a   For wicked and deceitful mouths are opened against me,
2b   speaking against me with lying tongues.
3a   Indeed, they beset me with words of hate,
3b   and attack me without cause.
4a   In return for my love they accuse me
4b   —but I am a prayer!
5a   So they reward me evil for good,
5b   and hatred for my love.

6a   (They say), "Appoint a wicked man against him;
6b   let an accuser stand on his right.
7a   When he is tried, let him be found guilty;
7b   let his prayer be counted as sin.
8a   May his days be few;
8b   may another seize his position!
9a   May his children be orphans,
9b   and his wife a widow.
10a   May his children wander about and beg;
10b   may they be driven out of the ruins they inhabit!
11a   May the creditor seize all that he has;
11b   may strangers plunder the fruits of his toil.
12a   May there be no one to do him a kindness,
12b   nor anyone to pity his orphaned children.
13a   May his posterity be cut off;
13b   may his name be blotted out in the second generation!
14a   May the iniquity of his fathers be remembered before YHWH,
14b   and do not let the sin of his mother be blotted out:
15a   Let them be before YHWH continually,
15b   and may their memory be cut off from the earth!
16a   For he did not remember to show kindness,
16b   but pursued the poor and needy
16c   and the brokenhearted to their death!
17a   He loved to curse; let curses come on him!
17b   He did not like blessing; may it be far from him!
18a   He clothed himself with cursing as his coat,
18b   it soaked into his body like water,
18c   like oil into his bones.

19a May it be like a garment that he wraps around himself,
19b   like a belt that he wears every day!"

20a This is what my accusers ask for me before YHWH,
20b   those who speak evil against my life.

21a But you, YHWH, Adonai,
21b   act on my behalf according to your name.
21c   Because your steadfast love is good, deliver me!
22a For I am poor and needy,
22b   and my heart shudders within me.
23a I am gone like a shadow at evening;
23b   I am shaken off like a locust.
24a My knees are weak through fasting;
24b   my body has become gaunt.
25a Indeed, I am an object of scorn to them;
25b   when they see me, they shake their heads.

26a Help me, YHWH, my God!
26b   Save me according to your steadfast love.
27a Let them know that this is your hand;
27b   that you, YHWH, have done it.
28a Let them curse, but you will bless.
28b   Let my assailants be put to shame; while your servant will be glad.
29a May my accusers be clothed with dishonor;
29b   may they be wrapped in their own shame as in a mantle.

30a With my mouth I will give great thanks to YHWH;
30b   I will praise him in the midst of the throng.
31a For he stands at the right hand of the needy,
31b   to save them from those who would condemn them to death!

This is another psalm that has fallen victim in toto to the shears of the reformers of the Liturgy of the Hours. If we think of the misuse of it practiced by the church's liturgists for many centuries, we might even say, Thank God!

What I have in mind is a twofold misuse of the psalm: One is its anti-Jewish application. In principle, that already began in the New Testament, where the figure of Judas Iscariot—an invention of anti-Jewish polemic—is fingered and cursed as the "fulfillment" of Psalm 109:8b, here read as a "prophecy":

> In those days Peter stood up among the believers (together the crowd numbered about one hundred twenty persons) and said, "Friends, the scripture had to be fulfilled, which the Holy Spirit through David foretold concerning Judas, who became a guide for

those who arrested Jesus—for he was numbered among us and was allotted his share in this ministry." (Now this man acquired a field with the reward of his wickedness; and falling headlong, he burst open in the middle and all his bowels gushed out. This became known to all the residents of Jerusalem, so that the field was called in their language Hakeldama, that is, Field of Blood.) "For it is written in the book of Psalms, 'Let his homestead become desolate, and let there be no one to live in it'; and 'Let another take his position of overseer' [cf. Ps. 109:8]!" (Acts 1:15–20, NRSV)

This application of Psalm 109 by the Lukan Peter found many zealous ecclesiastical imitators (especially Athanasius and Augustine), who then read the whole psalm as referring to Judas. For that reason, the title "Psalmus Ischarioticus" even crept into the designation of the psalm. "Judas" then very quickly became the prototype of "Jews," and so the Jews were cursed and damned in the name of the Davidic prophecy of Psalm 109. It was not infrequently the case that Psalm 109 was "prayed" as a divine legitimation of pogroms against the Jews.

The other misuse of Psalm 109 remained in some sense internal to the Christian community. There it was misapplied as a "prayer for death" of supposed or real enemies.[20] Just as, in popular liturgy, Masses for the Dead were recited (for a hefty price!) against the living, as a magical-sacramental means of hastening them, with God's help, into the great beyond, so also the Bible (especially the psalms) was used for magical purposes. Manuscripts offer detailed catalogues for the use of individual psalms in various situations. We know about the widespread practice of "praying people to death" with the aid of Psalm 109 primarily because of a dissertation presented in 1708 by Johann Friedrich Heine to the University of Helmstedt (which ultimately closed its doors after the University of Göttingen was founded in its vicinity in 1735). Heine writes on this subject, in part:

> In our time, when the clear light of the gospel penetrates all eyes, we must deeply lament that there are people so wholly surrendered to this kind of superstition. . . . Many believe that this psalm must be prayed without interruption for a whole year and nine days, morning and evening. . . . But if this enchantment is neglected even one time, it is thought that it will not fall upon the head of the enemy, and instead will turn back upon the one who prays it. The enemy must know nothing of the reading of the psalm; in addition, one must not greet him [or her] in the street or accept a greeting, and all sorts of other absurd customs derived from pagan superstition are in circulation.[21]

Heine also tells of a clergyman from Magdeburg who, because he was angry at a member of the city council, began and ended every sermon with

Psalm 109, directed against the magistrate he hated. When he was asked to stop this silly behavior, he threatened to expand the psalm by "putting it into action." We also know of this Christian abuse of Psalm 109 from Luther's writings (in fact, he in turn urged people to pray Count Moritz to death with the psalm) and those of Calvin, who says in his commentary on Psalm 109:6:

> All the more to be condemned is the sacrilege committed by the monks, especially the Franciscans, when they desecrate this psalm. For it is no secret that anyone who has a deadly enemy he [or she] wants to ruin employs one of these villains to recite the psalm daily against him [or her]. In France, I am aware that a noble lady had Franciscans in her employ in order to curse her only son in this way.[22]

This custom of attempting to "pray enemies to death" with Psalm 109 can be shown to have continued in Bavaria, Swabia, and Switzerland into the nineteeth century. The fact that this kind of abuse, on the one hand, finds "pegs" on which to hang itself (but not genuine causes!) in some expressions in the psalm, when they are wrongly understood, is something that must *also* be considered when posing the question about *whether* or *how* this psalm should be prayed. On the other hand, it is equally obvious that this "praying to death" not only collided with many other expressions in the same psalm, but with the overall meaning of the psalm itself.

In dealing with the psalm, we must first of all confront this *overall meaning*. Anyone who always reads the "Jewish" psalms with eyes that are continually on the lookout to detect "less than Christian" utterances in them will, of course, do the same with Psalm 109. W. Stärk, writing in the series "Die Schriften des Alten Testaments [The Old Testament Scriptures]," summarizes his verdict on Psalm 109 as follows:

> If we could erase the major central section of this psalm, verses 6–20, we would have one of the most tender prayers of petition that honest piety ever sent up to God out of the suffering of body and soul. But as it is, the prayer of the devout sinks down through the dreadful curses that are uttered against the persecutors in those verses, down into an immoral vengeance. However, it is these verses that give color to the psalm. It is a genuine imprecatory psalm and is not intended to be anything else. It is the duty of a responsible scholarly explication of this most unfortunate creation of Old Testament religious poetry to acknowledge that, and it is a poorly applied coverup to say that, while such curses are not in accord with the spirit of the New Testament, they are not without moral value and spiritual power because there is a divine energy in them, as there is in the curses and blessings of every human being who clings to God; or even to grasp at the foolish idea that verses 6ff. are, in fact, curses spoken against the devout person by the torturer.[23]

Because Alfons Deissler agrees with Stärk in rejecting the attempt to explain verses 6–19 as the quotation of curses and threats flung at the one who prays Psalm 109, he expresses serious reservations about Psalm 109 in his commentary on the book of Psalms:

> Our psalm is the most offensive example of the so-called "imprecatory psalms." . . . Jesus' saying about the duty to love even our enemies—in which the command of justice and mercy, already present in the old covenant, attains its highest possible development—and his corresponding example on the cross do not permit us to accept Psalm 109 in its literal sense as a prayer for Christians. Romans 12:17–21 also speaks clearly against it. However, it is difficult to bring verses 6–20 onto the level of a "no to sin and Satan." Therefore it would be best to drop them from the Christian psalter. Peter's use of verse 8 (Acts 1:20) is not a precedent for retaining them. . . . It is different with the complaints and pleas, and with the confession of confidence in being heard (1–5, 21–31). These fit well on the lips of Jesus, the most guiltless of all those falsely accused throughout the history of humanity. They can indeed be prayed by God's people of the new covenant, as the still living and still hated "Christ" (cf. John 15:18ff.).[24]

For exegetical, not apologetic reasons, I myself consider the so-called quotation hypothesis the most adequate explanation of the series of curses in verses 6–19, which are, in fact, shocking. A twofold function is achieved within the dynamic of the prayer when the one praying gives such a complete list, in verses 6–19, of the curses of the enemies directed against the devout person him- or herself. On the one hand, these words give a dramatic and tangible expression to the hopelessness and powerlessness of the one who prays. Here is an escalation of psychic and social terror that surrounds the one praying like a deadly, poisonous cloud. He or she holds up this quotation before God, in some sense as proof of his or her distress and the necessity that YHWH put an end to this business, "for your name's sake" (cf. v. 21). On the other hand, these humanly demeaning and blasphemous words of the enemies are, at the same time, a literary and theological contrast to the words of the one who prays in verses 1–5, 21–31. There is a polished artistry in the way these two worlds collide. This is political poetry as prayer (see chapter 3, "Poetic Prayers").

The following observations and considerations give particular support to the quotation hypothesis. Their persuasive power is cumulative:

1. That the enemies curse and accuse the one who prays is expressly stated in verse 28a.
2. The desire of the one praying for vengeance on the enemies is uncontestably expressed in verses 28b–29. This desire is positively mild in

comparison to the curses collected in verses 6–19; its aim is the sudden rupture of the nets of the enemies' violence, and that the enemies should stand "naked" and ashamed of their mean games. The difference in the language and motifs of the two "cursing passages" is more easily explained if the poetic dramaturgy is here bringing different voices to speech.

3. In verses 1–5 and verses 21–31, the praying person sees himself or herself confronted with a group of enemies (plural constructions); in contrast, the destructive desires expressed in verses 6–19 are directed against an *individual* (singular constructions). This is most easily explained if the one praying cries out against the enemies in verses 1–5, 21–31, while in verses 6–19 the words of the enemies are directed against the (individual) person praying the psalm.

4. It is frequently the case in the book of Psalms that a psalm of lament and petition cites the actual words of the enemies and the wicked, in order to give an especially vivid picture of their hubris and brutality (cf., among others, Pss. 3:3; 10:4, 6, 11, 13; 12:5; 13:5; 14:1).

5. It cannot be maintained against the quotation hypothesis that the psalm itself presents no introductory quotation formula (I have clearly inserted it in the translation above). What are incontestably direct speeches are often quoted in the psalms without introduction (e. g., Pss. 2:3; 14:4; 22:9; 28:7; 30:10–11; 32:8; 46:11; 50:7).

6. Verse 20 is a kind of colophon or "subtitle" to verses 6–19 as a summary of the opponents' speech and a transition to the emphatic cry of the devout person for YHWH's help. In fact, the new beginning in verse 21 would be rather peculiar if verses 6–19 had to be read as the *words of the one praying* against his or her enemies.

In particular, however, the quotation hypothesis recommends itself on the basis of the whole structure of the psalm. It is a cry for help by a person who is simply described as someone who is *persecuted and attacked*. The mortal threat to which he or she has become an innocent and defenseless victim is exposed in several dimensions (the question whether there is a perceptible growth of the psalm over time can here remain open): here we find public calumny and hostile threats, involvement in the processes of a corrupt justice system, social and economic ruin at the hands of the wealthy and powerful. All this is experienced as the lying and hatred of people who want to destroy the devout person and his or her family. In this extreme distress, he or she *will not and cannot* retaliate with the same weapons. Instead, the one who prays appeals to the God of mercy and blessing to save—to save the one against whom these enemies are fighting without cause, and who has practiced the love demanded by Leviticus 19 (cf. the echoes of Lev.

19:17–18 in v. 5). The devout one ruptures the vicious circle of violence with the cry, "In return for my love they accuse me—but I am a prayer!" This prayer is our very psalm itself! In it, the one who prays adjures YHWH to stand "at the right hand of the needy," to rescue the poor and to prove that YHWH is the one who has been revealed as the God of Exodus. Can this psalm really not be a prayer for Christians?

3

Toward a Hermeneutic of the Psalms of Enmity and Vengeance

In this chapter, we are not interested in a fundamentalist defense of the psalms of enmity and vengeance that are experienced as difficult or genuinely offensive, as if they must necessarily be retained because they are "the word of God" and "revelation." These psalms, rather, challenge us to examine and differentiate the heretofore unreflective manner of speaking about the Bible as "the word of God," which is therefore to be accepted in obedient faith. It is not a question of a considered apologetic that can and will explain away the offensiveness of these texts. And it is not a question of trying to place these texts, and the theology and anthropology they represent, at the center of our ecclesial and personal prayer. Instead, my concern is to describe the theological horizon within which these psalms originated in such a way as to remove the misunderstandings that arise *in us* when and because we hear these psalms too much in terms of our own feelings about life and our assimilation of the pseudo-theological clichés of the Christian tradition. I am also concerned to make them comprehensible as the *authentic prayers* of biblical people, so that they can be seen not only as challenges to our Christian prayer systems, but also as a genuine enrichment to them. The concrete implications of this will be sketched in chapter 4.

". . . To Judge the Living and the Dead"

Probably the most important thing we can say about God is that the world and history belong to *God,* and it is *God* who has the last word about history, as its "judge." At the same time, this is probably the statement that has occasioned the most misunderstanding, and continues to do so, whether it is given a narrow christological interpretation (as in the Christian creed: "He is seated at the right hand of God, the Father almighty; from there he will come to judge the living and the dead"), or whether it is heard as more strongly theocentric. These misunderstandings, in turn, are an obstacle to an appropriate understanding of the *biblical* language about God as judge and "avenger." The distortions of the article of faith about the final judgment have also been preserved in many depictions of the last judgment, and in Christian prayers whose structural hideousness far outstrips the violent perspective of the biblical psalms.

Joseph Ratzinger, in his *Introduction to Christianity,* gave a good summary of the traditional Christian misunderstandings:

> No one can deny that the article [of the creed] concerning judgment has at times assumed a form in the mind of Christians that, in practice, was bound to lead to the destruction of a fully-developed faith in the redemption and the promise of mercy. The example repeatedly cited is the profound contrast between *Maranatha* and *Dies irae.* Primitive Christianity, with its prayer, "Our Lord, come" (*Maranatha*), interpreted the return of Jesus as an event full of hope and joy; these early Christians yearned longingly towards it as the moment of the great fulfillment. To the Christians of the Middle Ages, on the other hand, that moment appeared as the terrifying "day of wrath" (*Dies irae*), in face of which human beings, in their pain and terror, will long to vanish away, and which they anticipate with fear and dread. The return of Christ is nothing but judgment, the day of the great accounting that threatens every individual. Such a view forgets something crucial, and Christianity is reduced, for all practical purposes, to moralism and robbed of that breath of hope and joy that is the true expression of its unique life.[1]

This distortion of the message about the judgment of *God,* whose sadistic and/or masochistic destructiveness continues to have its impact in pseudo-Christian threats and fantasies of hell found even today in authoritarian Catholic fundamentalist circles and in the Marian apocalyptic of Fatima—plaguing people with anxieties and neuroses—also (often unconsciously) stamps Christian reservations and prejudices about the psalms that speak of divine judgment or even cry out for it. We have suppressed in our Christian consciousness the idea that judgment is for the sake of justice, especially for those who are the victims of injustice, and that the purpose of this judgment is to restore everything "as it should be"—and even to confront the wicked with their injustice in such a way that they honor justice through their repentance. That is why we find it so difficult to recognize the historical perspective of the psalms of enmity and vengeance as a cry for justice and righteousness and a signal of hope against pseudo-religious fatalism and fanaticism, and thus to agree with it in principle. The kind of potential for hope that lies in this talk about judgment, and the amount of strength it affords for resistance, as well as for holding fast to one's own human worth, even when it is being trodden underfoot, was formulated in the magnificent (and unfortunately all too soon forgotten) "confession of hope" of the Synod of Würzburg in this way:

> Closely bound up with our hope for the resurrection of the dead is the Christian expectation of the judgment of God on our world and its history, at the end of time when the Son of Man returns. But can the message about God's judgment be articulated in any way as an expression of our hope? Certainly, it may contradict our own dreams of progress and harmony, which we so willingly combine with our ideas of "salvation." But at the same time, it expresses an idea that, as part of our Christian message, is full of promise: namely, the specifically Christian notion of the equality of all human beings. This does not end in a mere leveling, but exalts the equality of all persons in their practical responsibility for their lives before God; it also affirms an everlasting hope for those who suffer injustice. This Christian idea of equality aims at justice for all, and therefore does not cripple interest in a historical struggle to achieve that justice; instead, it repeatedly kindles our awareness of our responsibility for this justice. How else would we be able to stand before the judgment?
>
> Indeed, we must ask: have we in the church not often been responsible for obscuring this liberating meaning of the message about God's final judgment, because we have preached the word of judgment loudly and urgently to the weak and defenseless, while frequently our preaching has been too soft and half-hearted when directed to the powerful of this earth? And yet, if any word of our hope deserves to be acknowledged boldly, and especially before "governors and kings" (cf. Matt. 10:18), surely it is this one! Then it reveals all of its strength of consolation and encouragement: It speaks of the power of God to create justice; that our longing for justice does not expire in death; that not only is love stronger than death, but so is justice. Finally, it tells of the power of God to create justice that flings down death from its throne as the ruler of our conscience, and assures us that death does not set a seal on the lordship of the masters and the enslavement of the lowly. Shall we say that this is not a word of hope?—a word that makes us free to stand up for this justice, whether it is convenient or not? Is this not an incentive for us to resist situations of injustice that cry out to heaven? Is this not a measure that forbids us to compromise in any way with injustice, and continually obligates us to scream against it, because not to do so is to revile our own hope?[2]

It is evident in the psalms themselves that in Israel, faith in a God who, as judge, will accomplish and restore justice marked the dividing line between "the wicked" and "the righteous." The "wicked" menace and bring ruin to "the poor and needy" through the many practices of their daily violence, not least because they can only ridicule the idea of a God whose judgment will show concern for the weak and the marginalized. This is expressed particularly in the blasphemous speeches placed on the lips of the wicked:

> In the pride of their countenance the wicked say,
>   "God will not seek it out";
>   all their thoughts are, "There is no God."
>
> . . . .
>
> They think in their heart, "God has forgotten,
>   he has hidden his face, he will never see it."
>
> . . . .
>
> Why do the wicked renounce God,
>   and say in their hearts, "You
>   will not call us to account"?
>   (Ps. 10:4, 11, 13, NRSV)

> Fools say in their hearts, "There is
>   no God."
>   (Ps. 14:1 = 53:1, NRSV)

> [My enemies] say, "Pursue and seize that person
>   whom God has forsaken,
>   for there is no one to deliver."
>   (Ps. 71:11, NRSV)

> And they say, "How can God know?
>   Is there knowledge in the Most High?"
>   (Ps. 73:11, NRSV)

The cries for help or vengeance in the psalms are not about lesser or greater conflicts that could be resolved by wise generosity on the part of the one praying, or through "love of neighbor." Instead, those who pray these psalms are shouting out their suffering because of injustice and the hubris of the violent. They confront their own God with the mystery of evil and the contradiction represented by evil persons in a world that is in the care of God. This is not the trivial complaint of people whose thoughts and cares are only for themselves and their own advantage. The passion of these psalms arises from the fundamental conviction that justice must be done—at least, it must be done by a God who has created the world as a "house to live in" for all creatures, a God who will arise over that world as "the sun of justice" that drives out evil and brings salvation to those in peril of death. The fact that the psalms cry to God as judge, of course, does not dispense the courts of this world of their obligation to accomplish right and justice. But these cries give voice to the painful reality that human judges and courts are insufficient to establish perfect justice.

Gottfried Bachl, dogmatic theologian of Salzburg, has very impressively explained why it is that, in both the Old *and* New Testaments, so central a message as that about God's judgment is good news (gospel!). First he illustrates, by means of an example, what *judgment* means:

> On 8 March 1988, German television presented a film in which the destruction of the little French village of Oradour-sur-Glane was brought to light again. On 10 June 1944, an SS division retaliated against the French Resistance by completely destroying this settlement. In the process, some six hundred men, women, and children were burned or shot to death.
>
> One of the officers who commanded this liquidation later lived in the German Democratic Republic as a respected employee in a business establishment, a beloved father and grandfather to his family, attached by the most tender affections to his grandchildren. In 1980, thirty-six years after his deed, he was arrested, prosecuted, and sentenced to life imprisonment. A reporter was able to visit him in prison and conducted a long interview with him, during which he wept repeatedly. When the reporter asked, "Why are you crying now?" he answered, "Because I have been so happy, and now it ends this way." The journalist continued, "Did you ever weep over the children, women, and men you killed that day?" "No," he said. "Did it never occur to you that you had done a terrible injustice to those people?" His answer: "No, not as long as I was free. Everything was quite normal. But now I often think that there must have been something wrong, that I was involved in it myself somehow, that probably the whole thing was wrong."
>
> Tears, and a slight beginning of remorse, even a hint of recognition of the facts only began for this man when *the judgment of the court* saw to it that he had to face up to the event, so that the deed came back to him, touching him in body and spirit. Now he was in the process of awakening from his obtuse, happy captivity in his own well-being and self-satisfaction; now he was beginning to be a human being who sees what he has done. It was judgment that made that possible for him.[3]

From this confrontation between a human being and a human court of
justice we can discern what can and must occur in the confrontation before
the "judgment of God"—and not only beyond the grave and at the end of
history, but, as Bachl shows, even here and now:

> The current of our history does not issue in justice, but in the ques-
> tion: Where will it happen? Will it ever appear in its true, compre-
> hensive form? No court, not even the judgment of all humanity, will
> be adequate to the things that, even now, the people in Bosnia are
> doing to one another at a distance from us, and others here at home
> in the intimate circles of their families. What happens in the world
> of humanity is from its very beginning a cry for God's judgment.
> And the first response to that cry that is found in the gospel, the *good
> news*, is:
>
> The stream of events will not run on forever, over blood and
> victims, goodness, evil, innocence and justice. *God* will put an end
> to the course of history and will make clear that there is a difference
> between justice and injustice, and that this difference must be
> demonstrated. God will seek out the buried victims, the forgotten,
> starved children, the dishonored women, and God will find the hid-
> den doers of these deeds. God will gather all of them before God's
> eternal, holy will for the good, so that all *must* see how it stands with
> their lives.
>
> That is what the gospel says about the great sweep of world his-
> tory. But it also speaks the word of the judge directly to each indi-
> vidual. The book of Genesis begins with a scene of judgment. God
> calls to the human being, "Adam, where are you?" Adam has hid-
> den, and is now brought forth. Then follows the conversation that
> seeks him out in his hidey-hole, his excuses and self-concealments.
> All the clothes are stripped from his body, so that he stands forth
> naked and real, and knows, "It is I," and no one else.
>
> Conversations like these that strip people bare are also com-
> mon enough with Jesus: in his encounter with the prostitute (Luke
> 7:36–50), with the tax collector Zacchaeus (Luke 19:1–10), with
> the woman at Jacob's well (John 4:1–26). What happens in these
> judgment dialogues can be expressed in modern language as fol-
> lows: Judgment is the way God helps human beings to self-discov-
> ery, it is liberation from the delusion of innocence, awakening
> from the sleep of conscience, release from life's lie. Because this
> help comes from God, it is unavoidable, efficient, painful and final
> in a healing way, occurring at the end of a human life, in death. In
> this way the human being gains himself or herself completely, be-
> comes genuine, capable of loving, and ready to receive the full
> presence of God.
>
> There are enough moments in this life in which we feel that we
> need this help, where we hope for it more than we fear it, because
> we sense that it will respond to the hunger we feel for truth, al-

though it is usually buried in cowardice; because we expect that it will realize that truth in us, in spite of our desire to be left in peace.[4]

That is the horizon within which the psalms cry to and for God, as we summarized in an example in chapter 1 of this book under the heading "Unpleasant and Repulsive Psalms":

LORD, God to whom vengeance belongs,
 God to whom vengeance belongs, appear!
Rise up, you judge of the world;
 repay the arrogant as they deserve!
     (Ps. 94:1–2, Unrevised Luther version)

A God of Vengeance After All?

Does not Psalm 94, just quoted, show after all that this judge in the psalms is understood as an "avenger"? Are not the hopes for destruction that the psalms fling against the wicked proof that the good news of God's judgment is more a release of human desires for vengeance than a curbing of them? Is not this destructive violence against enemies that is here expected and implored of God a constitutive aspect of God's own person? In short, is the trust in God we find so impressive in these psalms not so intertwined with desire for vengeance that what we have here is a hidden, but extremely dangerous, sacralization of aggression and violence? Is not the idea of the wrath of God, which appears especially and frequently in connection with biblical depictions of judgment in both testaments, a gigantic warning signal against any theologizing apologetic for the potential violence underlying the message of judgment?

An initial attempt to answer these questions must begin with semantics. It will not furnish a solution to the troubling problem itself, but it can liberate us from unnecessary misunderstandings. Some of the rejection of these psalms is, among other things, a problem of linguistic usage and of translation (on this, cf. below, chapter 4).

The problem of language was already implicitly visible when we presented (see chapter 1, "Unpleasant and Repulsive Psalms") the different translations in which, for example, the address to God in Psalm 94:1 appears. In the unrevised Luther version it reads:

"God *to whom vengeance belongs*, appear!"

whereas in the revised Luther version and *Einheitsübersetzung* it is:

"You God *of retaliation*, appear!"

compare with the NRSV:

"You God *of vengeance*, shine forth!"

and Martin Buber writes:

"God *of punishments,* appear!"

If we look at other translations, the variety is still greater:

"You God *of avenging,* appear!"
(N. H. Tur-Sinai)

"*Avenging power,* appear!"
(Leopold Zunz)

"God *of vengeance,* appear!"
(Zürcher Bibel)

The fact that the three Jewish translations (by Buber, Tur-Sinai, and Zunz) are distinguished by their greater linguistic variety from the rather standardized Christian translations signals an initial phenomenon in the biblical texts that we cannot pass over in superficial fashion. At this point, the psalm uses the plural *neqamot* (singular: *neqama*), which Buber represents with "punishments" and Tur-Sinai and Zunz with verbs of action. It is thus not a matter of making a statement about the nature of God, but about God's way of acting (which Luther also tries to retain with the translation "to whom vengeance belongs").

The second special feature is the significance of the Hebrew word itself. That this can no longer be translated as "vengeance" is evident, first of all, from the spectrum of meanings that words like "vengeance" or "revenge" have in English, and secondly from the context in which the Hebrew words *neqama* (noun) or *naqam* (verb) are used in the Hebrew Bible.

Jürgen Ebach describes the semantic problem as follows:

> What exactly is "vengeance"? One unabridged dictionary of the German language ("Duden") gives the following definition: "personal retaliation, often emotionally motivated, against a deed experienced as malicious, and especially as personal injustice; paying back of an injustice, a humiliation, defeat, insult, and similar things." The *dtv* dictionary places the accent differently: "retaliation for an injustice suffered, by one's own hand (blood vengeance), as well as the feelings of hatred and the emotions that motivate it."* Vengeance is thus the expression of an emotion, and as praxis it is an action outside the rules of legal procedure. As a feeling, vengeance is saddled with the odium of something uncontrolled; revengeful feelings are regarded as immoral, even though under-

---

* *Translator's note:* Cf. *The American Heritage Dictionary of the English Language* (Boston, New York, and London: Houghton Mifflin, 1992): "Infliction of punishment in return for a wrong committed; retribution."

standable in certain circumstances. In our legal systems, the practice of vengeance is outside the law; the state's monopoly on violence and the associated demand that there be no retaliation that is not subject to the rules of the justice system exclude acts of vengeance from the repertoire of justified reactions to injustice suffered. Vengeance has been replaced by punishment or, in the case of conflicts in civil law, a regulated process of compensation.[5]

When those who pray call to their God as the righteous judge, they avert "vengeance" from themselves. It is not some irrational, wildly abusive God to whom they cry (one before whom they themselves would be in fear!). They appeal to a God who, as the God of justice, considers, decides, and punishes, this last not out of a pleasure in punishment, but in order to restore and defend the damaged order of law. The analogue in the background here is precisely not uncontrolled or secret vengeance, but the public intervention of a legitimate, constituted authority that makes its decisions according to legal principles and whose intention is to protect and advance the common good through a legitimate imposition of punishment.

It is true that our English words "vengeance" and "revenge" derive etymologically from Latin *vindicare*, which refers to the entering of a legal claim,* so that there are connotations of law and justice here as well. Still, neither our everyday language nor the juridical application of "vengeance" and "revenge" takes account of that context (for example, killing for revenge counts as murder!). There may be different opinions on the question whether translating the word here as "punishments"† (Martin Buber) provides a solution to the semantic problem; in any case, that word (in German) has acquired such an archaic flavor that it calls us to reflection.

At all events, the contexts in which God is called upon or appears as a punishing and avenging judge carry a great deal of emotion with them. The "pleas for punishment" on the part of those praying are themselves marked by a quite unbridled emotion, because they express the deeply wounded feelings of the suffering and their doubt about "God and the world." Therefore the public system of justice remains only an analogue for what is at stake in talk about God as judge/"avenger"/savior. The appeal and the trust of those praying, in fact, depend essentially on the presupposition that God is *personally* touched by injustice, and is even called into question by it—and that God must bring about justice "for the sake of God's own name." To that extent, God is not at all a nonparticipating, neutral representative of an independent court of justice. Precisely because God is a living God, those who pray seek to call their God forth from aloofness and move this God to take

---

Translator's note: The author refers to the German word *Rache* and cognate terms, etymologically derived from *Recht* and *rechten*.
†*Translator's note:* The German word is *Ahndung*.

sides! God is not only to exercise the office of judge, but in doing so to communicate *God's own self*.

For that very reason, this God can also forgo the punishment that is deserved, even when the judgment and punishment have already been announced. That is the theological message of the book of Jonah. Under that theological reservation stand *all* the pleas for punishment and destruction directed to YHWH, whether or not those praying are willing that it should be so. The cry that urges God *tua res agitur* ("This is your business, God!") is comprehensive: It is also *God's* business that divine judgment "does not desire the death of sinners, but rather that they should turn from their way and live" (cf. Ezek. 18:23; 33:11).

What is said about the wrath of God is also to be understood in this context. Certainly, on the one hand, this language emphasizes the personal aspect of God's responsibility for the world in mythical and anthropomorphic language and imagery. The wrath of God is closely connected with God's "zeal for holiness," which binds God, and God's divine identity, with God's people and creation. To this extent, God's wrath is, on the other hand, a political-juristic category closely connected with the biblical concept of covenant. The Egyptologist Jan Assmann has described this specifically Israelite category of divine wrath as follows:

> This wrath is a specifically political emotion. It is gradually attributed to YHWH along with the role of king that YHWH assumes over Israel. This wrath is determined not by the irrational passions of a "wilderness demon," as was previously thought to be the case, but quite the opposite: it is the highly cultured idea of justice that is controlling here. It is the wrath of the judge who intervenes to save, and the wrath of the ruler that touches the vassals. Idolatry and oppression evoke the wrath of God, and both are offenses against the covenant made with God. Idolatry means falling away to other lords, and offends the contractual character of the covenant; oppression means turning away from the law that makes free, and offends against the divine rule of justice.
>
> This political interpretation of divine wrath goes back to antiquity. Lactantius devoted an entire book to the wrath of God. The problem, as it then appeared, was connected with the idea of divine affectivity. The Greek word for "affect" is *pathos*, which also means "suffering." In Greek thinking, affects or emotions were "suffered," and were essentially "passive." Can God suffer? Philosophical, and especially Stoic, monotheism in antiquity postulated the absolute perfection and therefore the impassibility of God. Lactantius insists, against this, that wrath does not belong to the *essence* (*natura*) of God, but to God's *role*, God's *imperium* or *dominium;* it represents a form of God's preserving, saving, and justice-creating relationship

to the world. Wrath and mercy are mutually conditioned and both follow, as a matter of logical necessity, from the idea of divine relationship with the world. Anyone who denies God these affects, denies God's relationship to the world and makes God a *deus otiosus* (functionless God), to whom no worship is due. A God who knows no wrath requires no cult: *religio esse non potest ubi metus nullus est* ["religion cannot exist where there is no fear"]. Wrath, love, and mercy are attributes of the divine office of judging and are indispensable for keeping the world in motion. . . .

God is not unpolitical. This thesis is one of the basic propositions of every political theology. On this point, Egypt and Israel are also in complete agreement. The difference lies only in the fact that in Egypt God—the singular is fully appropriate here—hands over governance, that is, the role of ruling and judging the world, to the king, who represents God in this role, while in Israel it is God who exercises the role immediately and in person.[6]

When the psalms cry, "Pour out your wrath on my/our enemies," they may evoke protest and rejection among our modern contemporaries, to whom the religious-historical origins of the category of wrath and knowledge of its specifically Israelite character remain a mystery, but simply to eliminate such phrases would reduce the biblical God to a spectator uninterested in this world, or to a *deus otiosus,* and thus to an *idea* of God that, moreover, would be lacking in every kind of social-critical potential.

The irritating and provocative talk about a "God of punishments" and the "wrath of God" says something, at the outset, about the violent and wretched state of society and the world—and that this situation is not created by God, nor can it be legitimated or tolerated as something God-given—not by us as human beings, and certainly not by God. The "psalms of enmity" intend to, and must, remind us of that.

A Dynamic World Image and
a Realistic View of the World

Behind the demand for divine judgment and the appeal to God's responsibility for God's people and world stands a dynamic image of the world that "thinks of" creation and the life of the nations in a permanent back-and-forth between chaos and cosmos. It is true that, in biblical thought, chaos and cosmos are not equal realities in a dualistic sense. At the same time, however, chaos is seen as a violent force out of which "creation" was fashioned (cf. Gen. 1; Wis. 11:17–18). There is even the idea that YHWH created the chaos (cf. Isa. 45:7; Prov. 8:23–24). This chaos permanently surrounds and pervades the cosmos, but it is resisted (cf. Isa. 51:9–10; Pss. 74 and 89; Job 26:40–41) and regulated (cf. Pss. 46, 48, 93, 104). This

conception of chaos, which Israel shares with its neighbors, brings into realistic focus the disturbing, daily experienced endangerment of the cosmos,
and its contradiction to the biblical talk about God who has created all
things good. On the other hand, its concept of a personal creator-God offers a beginning point for influencing this chaos-cosmos struggle by means
of an appeal—that is, through the psalms that are constructed as prayers to
God.

These psalms are a form of human struggle against chaos—a struggle simultaneously *against* and *with* God. They are neither the result of dogmatic
reflection nor the expression of higher or lower ethical sensibility. They are
the mirror and the articulation of fear and the state in which those who pray
now find themselves and/or in which they see others. In this, they are the
expression of a passionate conviction that this situation contradicts what
they believe and hope about the reality of God. Thus these psalms are intended to be a challenge, a calling forth of God to fight against chaos. To
that end, they also introduce the "curses of the enemy," which from the perspective of form criticism are seen to be derived from the ritual of cursing.
With the quasi-magical power of these curses, they hope to frighten "evil"
and liberate creative and healing powers; in particular, they desire to call
God forth from reserved withdrawal.

It may be that the directness of the challenge to God and the certainty it
expresses that God must be at work in history and society form the real
provocation of these psalms for a Christianity whose belief in God has ex-
hausted its historical potential in soteriology or postponed it to an afterlife
by a privatist and spiritualizing attitude. Here the shrill tones of the psalms
of enmity can serve to shock Christianity out of the well-regulated slumber
of its structural amnesia about God.

Even if the magical and mythical origin of the dynamic worldview that
shapes the psalms (which, of course, should not be misunderstood in the
sense of a development toward something more perfect) brings with it certain limitations, its "serviceability" for daily life can scarcely be overesti-
mated. I see this primarily under the following four aspects:

1. No matter how much "the enemies" in the psalms are expressions of
   chaos, and no matter how much their actions are represented in the
   symbolic imagery of a counter-world or a mysterious structural super-
   power, these "enemies" are never mythicized or demonized. Even
   when the struggle between chaos and cosmos is portrayed, as in Psalm
   58, as a conflict among gods, it is displaced from heaven to earth and
   connected to concrete social reality (cf. chapter 2, "Psalm 58: A Cry
   for Right and Justice"). That shows us the realistic worldview of these
   psalms. They uncover the mechanisms of violence as actions and
   strategies emanating from concrete human beings and institutions.

With their often excessive imagery they name the terror that open and veiled violence brings about. Thus they are the necessary barb acting against the temptation to minimize or ignore repressive and destructive violence.

2. To the extent that those who pray the psalms not only condemn violence when they themselves are immediately oppressed and threatened by it, but uncover it as a structural distortion of the earth as the abode of life, something that is offensive to God, they demystify every ideology that presents itself all too enthusiastically as promising happiness and liberation.

3. These psalms can and will make obvious the web of violence presented, especially for the weak, the sick, the suffering, and those under attack by a hostile environment (or one that is felt to be hostile). With their concrete expressions of fear and pain, they bring that pain to the center of ordinary religious and social life. They are the expression of that sensitivity to suffering that is constitutive for biblical piety, and for any way of life that is shaped by the Bible. Johannes Baptist Metz, in his programmatic final lecture at Münster, explained why Christianity must begin again to take lessons from these psalms:

In recent years I have repeatedly asked myself what happened to Christianity when (and by the way, it was the only one of the major monotheistic religions to do this) it became a theology. What moved me to this was not an interest in a nonconceptual denial of the differentiated profile of Christianity; I was not interested in *simplified relationships,* but in the question whether the way in which it became a theology did not cause something to be repressed, forgotten, or silenced that is indispensable, especially today, for the verbal and moral authority of Christianity. In my opinion, in the process of this theologizing Christianity lost its sensitivity to suffering, or, to put it in theological terms, its sensitivity to theodicy; that is, it ceased to be troubled by the question of justice for innocent sufferers. In the same moment, it lost its sensitivity to time; that is, it ceased to be troubled by the question of the end of time: How long? *Maranatha!* This two-in-one loss is ordinarily not regarded as loss; instead, it is seen as a victory, the victory of theological reason, and above all as a theological victory over the Jewish traditions in Christianity. But in my opinion it lies at the root of the present crisis of authority for Christianity, in face of which—I am repeating myself—all other church crises in Christianity are secondary in nature.

Christian God-talk has lost its sensitivity to suffering. From the beginning, Christian theology attempted to keep its distance from the troubling question of justice for innocent sufferers by transforming it into a question of the redemption of sinners. The theodicy question, the problem of God in face of the profound history of the world's suffering, the pain of *God's* world, became a soteriological circle; it was soteriologically encoded—and not without evil consequences. Christianity transformed itself from a morality of suffering to a morality of sin; a Christianity sensitive to suffering became a Christianity sensitive to sin. Primary attention was given, not to the suffering of creation, but to its guilt. Christian theology became, above all, a heuristic of guilt feelings and anxiety over sin. This hobbled its sensitivity to the suffering of the righteous and obscured the biblical vision of the great righteousness of God—and yet, in face of that righteousness, the hunger and thirst of everyone has to be accounted for.[7]

4. Because the psalms of enmity express sensitivity to suffering in light of the misfortune *of others* within *their own* address to God in prayer, those who pray them are inevitably faced with the question of *their own* complicity in the web of violence—and not primarily within the moral category of sin, but within the *theological* category of obstacles placed in the way of the realm of God's justice and of life. In this way, these psalms avoid the fantasy of innocence and, not least by their continually repeated questions, "How long?" and "Why?" they place those who pray them under the same pressure of time embodied in a good Jewish petition in the "Our Father": "Your kingdom come!"

Poetic Prayers

What is true of the psalms as a whole must be considered and savored in a special way in the psalms of enmity: They are poetry, and as poetry they live out of and within their manifold imagery, in which they concentrate experiences and attempt to convey them in their depth and enduring vitality, and in which they paint and invoke the dramatic anxieties and erupting agonies, as well as the brutality of hostile power and their hopes for the intervention of the God who can put an end to this vicious circle of violence. Those who are familiar with poetry, literature, and painting will not find it difficult to enter into the psalms as poetry. But those who are negatively preconditioned or have their ears corrupted by the generally unpoetic language of the literature of ordinary Christian prayer will have to sensitize themselves and open their ears in order to achieve access to this language, especially since some of the images can only be understood in depth on the basis of knowledge of their cultural and religious origins. Therefore one must "see one's way into" this world of imagery—just as with any poetry!

Those who understand the imagery of the psalms as a medium of poetic expression, and who desire to awaken the experiences and hopes entangled in the images themselves, cannot stop with a mere comprehension of their content. It is very important to appreciate the form of the image in its compositional technique as well. Sometimes there is a play on individual elements of the image, and sometimes collages and cascades of images are placed alongside one another or intermingled, held in tension, and even deliberately designed to shock. Sometimes a psalm is based on a single major image, and at other times we find an artistic mingling of imagery and conceptual language. No matter how the technique of imagery is executed in the individual psalms, the source of their poetic power and fascination may well open itself with ever new surprises to those who surrender themselves to it: It is precisely in their language of images that the psalms are open to the many concrete realizations that life brings in its wake, and creatively available for the demands of each day: to find a way to take up, again and again, the struggle against violence and suffering, in a prayerful stance of appeal to God to come forward and to act.

The psalms of enmity are nourished primarily by the tension between the destructive and constructive images they contain. Here images of fear and hope are so intensely woven together that an immersion in this world of imagery can release a positive and even therapeutic power within us. The approach to poetry associated with depth psychology has very properly called our attention to this dimension of the language of the psalms.

In the first place, there are images of fear that are very similar to those in our dreams:

> Rising water, sinking in the mire, drought and burning thirst, slipping and falling, ravenous beasts and overwhelmingly powerful enemies. . . . But they have this advantage over the fleeting shapes in our dreams: they are of a different consistency, deeply impressive and readily retained, and they can withstand a thoroughly substantial and sober analysis. These are signs that, like those in our dreams, correspond directly to our fears and desires. . . . We are talking about a linguistic symbol whose unique character must be described somewhat as follows: It unites the reality of our external experience in a lasting manner with the world of our internal images; it points simultaneously to both these realities, and thus keeps them semantically in parallel.[8]

In these images, our anonymous and elementary fears can find expression and thus lose their destructiveness.

> What does it mean to speak of enemies, if not to speak of our own fears? My enemy in the full sense is always that which makes me afraid, and the reverse is also true: when I am afraid, I see myself surrounded by enemies, human or superhuman; indeed, I can cre-

ate enemies for myself by projecting my fears. But when it is a question of genuine fears, how else can we speak of them than by seeking
freedom from them with all the passion we have, and that also means
seeking liberation from those who are the cause of those fears?[9]

This is exactly what happens in the psalms, often with primitive images
whose healing and liberating power is strengthened by the fact that, while
on the one hand they express an action of God, on the other hand their in-
tent is to help the praying subject to achieve independent selfhood. One
can even read these psalms as programs for self-realization. That God places
the feet of the fear-beset person who prays on solid ground, leads him or
her forth into open space, makes the darkness light, draws her or him forth
like a bucket filled with good spring water for others—these are images that
can move us to walk upright in the midst of chaos-arousing fears.

The fact that the so-called psalms of vengeance are *poetic* prayers distin-
guishes them from insistent complaint and propagandistic rhetoric. As poetry, most of these psalms hold to that narrow dividing line of discretion
that separates a genuine work of art, despite its immediacy, from embar-
rassing directness or nonexpressive mannerism.

The poetic power of these psalms is expressed primarily in their function
as lament and accusation. Because lament has largely disappeared from our
Christian prayer literature, it is not surprising that many Christians react
with bewilderment to these psalms of lament and accusation, although Jesus himself died shouting out the psalmist's indictment against God, "My
God, why have you forsaken me?" (Ps. 22:2 = Mark 15:34). It seems that
many Christians, and the church's official liturgists, in expelling lament
from our culture of prayer, are following what Martin Luther said on this
subject:

> If one were to transfer to us that which occurred in Christ, in all its
> elements and in the same way, it would be a blasphemy and mur-
> muring, whereas in him it was nothing but, in a certain sense, a shat-
> tering of weak nature, which, however, was similar in all things to
> our blasphemy and murmuring![10]

Precisely the depiction of Jesus' death on the cross in the passion story according to Mark contradicts this and gives lament its full "human rights,"
when the centurion is heard to say, in response to Jesus' cry, "Truly, *this man*
was the Son of God!" (Mark 15:39). If we note how the passion account has
consistently narrated the death scene in terms of the cry of anguish in Psalm
22:2, but also that the sequence of textual elements from Psalm 22 woven
into Mark 15 runs contrary to the sequence in the psalm itself and aims directly at the initial verse of the psalm, it will be obvious that Mark's intention is to blend out the hopeful conclusion of Psalm 22.[11] Against the back-

ground of the idea of Jesus as the "suffering righteous one" that shapes Mark 15, Psalm 22:2 in the mouth of Jesus is the accusation that holds open the question of theodicy: In an accusatory clinging to God when everything speaks *against* God, "this man" is found to have been "truly the Son of God" (Mark 15:39).

As poetic prayers, the psalms of vengeance are a passionate clinging to God when everything really speaks *against* God. For that reason they can rightly be called *psalms of zeal,* to the extent that in them passion for God is aflame in the midst of the ashes of doubt about God and despair over human beings. These psalms are the expression of a longing that evil, and evil people, may not have the last word in history, for this world and its history belong to God. Thus, to use theological terminology, these psalms are realized theodicy: They affirm God by surrendering the last word *to God.* They give *to God* not only their lament about their desperate situation, but also the right to judge the originators of that situation. They leave *everything* in God's hands, even feelings of hatred and aggression.

These psalms do not arise from the well-tempered psychological state of people from whom every scrap of sensitivity and emotion has been driven out. On the contrary, they are serious about the fundamental biblical conviction that in prayer we may say everything, literally everything, if only we say it to GOD, who is our father and mother. We have, in the meantime, learned from psychology that suppressed fears and repressed aggression do not overcome violence, but multiply it. What is necessary is that we learn to live with fears and aggressions by bringing them to consciousness and acting against their destructiveness. The psalms do not repress all this; they express it before GOD and place it in GOD's hands. Those who suffer injustice and sin as the opposites of love, and who therefore cry to GOD, in order that GOD will put an end to violence and contempt for human beings, are not prevented by this from living solidarity and love in concrete interaction with other human beings. Those who pray the psalms of zeal do not do so with blind eyes, but seeing, trusting that GOD will have the last word and that God's love is always greater than God's justice. Anyone who is agitated by the psalms of violence in this frame of mind has understood them at least a little.

The psalms of violence certainly belong among the songs of which Günter Eich says (in his radio play, "Träume"):

> Do what is useless, sing the songs
> that no one expects to hear from your mouth!
> Be inconvenient, be the sand,
> and not the grease in the gears of the world.

Those who sing these songs sing them as a cry for change and a melody of longing for a world without tears, usually in melancholy because this world will never exist without tears. Therefore they sing them as songs of protest and struggle. All of this harmonizes as a powerful song of resistance against the thin melodies that sing of a life of indifferent self-satisfaction and idyllic surrender to God. The song of the psalms of zeal tries to protect us from sinking into the banality of life, a life without secrets, and it does so by the very shrillness and scariness of its tone poems!

The Psalms of Vengeance: A Revelation of God?

Much of what we have said thus far about understanding the psalms of enmity will certainly meet with agreement. But the fundamental problem remains: That people in extreme situations of suffering and powerlessness, faced with mighty enemies, should cry out their distress and wish that their enemies should be shamed or even destroyed may appear tolerable, perhaps even acceptable, as an expression and consequence of the human limitations to which we are all subject. But that this should happen in prayer, and that God should be called upon to prove God's very identity by engaging in violence; that this is in sacred scripture, which we call the revelation of God, and that such prayers are even recommended to us in the name of God—should there not be a massive objection raised against this, at least on the part of a critical Christian theology? On the threshold of the third millennium, must we not finally apply all our strength to minimize the potential for violence? Is it not high time that at least the great religions of humanity self-critically uncover *all* the violent perspectives in their own traditions, and move against them by a consistent nonviolence, especially in their official texts?

With these last questions, one thing at least is certainly clear: This is not specifically a problem for Judaism, so that Christianity could merely withdraw from the affair by asserting that violent perspectives are simply a heritage of Judaism from which it has not yet sufficiently liberated itself. With respect to the psalms of violence, this is the expressed or implied prejudice inherent in all the positions that reject these psalms as "less than Christian," "unchristian," and "pre-Christian" (on this, see chapter 1, "Protest and Rejection in the Name of Christianity"). It is so obvious that a classification such as "violence, God of violence = Old Testament, Judaism" and "nonviolence, God of nonviolence = New Testament, Christianity" corresponds neither to the biblical texts nor to history that one can only be astonished that these vapid clichés are still put forward. In new variations (although only as a rehash of the thesis first developed by Marcion), this position is advocated by theologians who explain the violent expressions that are found in the New Testament, and even placed on the lips of the biblical Jesus, as typically Old Testament–Jewish distortion and covering up of the original message of Jesus by the New Testament authors, so that the task at hand would be to finally and consistently "de-judaize" Christianity.[12] The "new wine" of love and rejection of violence has to be liberated from the "old wineskins" in which Jesus' Jewish disciples had stored it.[13]

That on the one hand the antitheses Old/New Testaments and Judaism/Jesus are contrary to the biblical text, and that, on the other hand, the violent texts of the Bible are in tension with others that are critical of violence, not only in the New Testament but also (and perhaps more pointedly) in the Old Testament, presents us—along with the insight that the problem of religion and violence is posed by *all* religions—with a starting point from which we can begin to approach our question.

That *both testaments* appeal for the violent power of God *and* for an end to violence recalls for us the fundamental theological truth that the Bible is not revelation in the sense of an immediate, verbal communication from God, but is *"the word of God in human words."*[14] This fundamental axiom has far-reaching consequences for the hermeneutics of biblical texts.

The basic consequence is that any fundamentalist treatment of these texts is excluded. Such a treatment appears in two mutually exclusive forms: Either *all* the texts are defended as equally normative, on the basis of a fundamentalist conception of revelation ("Let the word of God stand!"), or individual texts must be excluded as incompatible with the biblical claim to be "the revelation of God." On the basis of this kind of fundamentalist approach, a whole series of texts from both the Old Testament and New Testament would have to be eliminated. Let me mention three examples:

What Paul says about marriage in 1 Corinthians (which was presented by many theologians over the centuries as normative for Christians, and "inspired" many official church documents) is simply not acceptable as the "literal" word of God:

> Now concerning the matters about which you wrote: "It is well for a man not to touch a woman." But because of cases of sexual immorality, each man should have his own wife and each woman her own husband. The husband should give to his wife her conjugal rights, and likewise the wife to her husband. For the wife does not have authority over her own body, but the husband does; likewise the husband does not have authority over his own body, but the wife does. Do not deprive one another except perhaps by agreement for a set time, to devote yourselves to prayer, and then come together again, so that Satan may not tempt you because of your lack of self-control. This I say by way of concession, not of command. I wish that all were as I myself am. But each has a particular gift from God, one having one kind and another a different kind. (1 Cor. 7:1–7, NRSV)

Analogously, in a fundamentalist understanding of revelation one would have to refuse the name "revelation" to many texts about war and destruction in the Old Testament (even if, or perhaps we should say *because* such texts were understood, in the course of the church's history, and especially in the context of mission, for example in South Africa and Latin America, as a biblical divine "command," with dreadful consequences for the original religions of those regions). Let me quote, as a brief example, some passages from Deuteronomy 7, where the theology of the love (!) of God for Israel developed in that book is simultaneously connected with some hideous fantasies of destruction:

> When YHWH, your God, brings you into the land that you are about to enter and occupy, and he clears away many nations before you— the Hittites, the Girgashites, the Amorites, the Canaanites, the Perizzites, the Hivites, and the Jebusites, seven nations mightier and more numerous than you—and when YHWH, your God, gives them over to you and you defeat them, then you must utterly destroy them. Make no covenant with them and show them no mercy. Do not intermarry with them, giving your daughters to their sons, for that would turn away your children from following me, to serve other gods. Then the anger of YHWH would be kindled against you, and he would destroy you quickly. But this is how you must deal with them: break down their altars, smash their pillars, hew down their sacred poles, and burn their idols with fire. For you are a people holy to the Lord your God; the Lord your God has chosen you out of all the peoples on earth to be his people, his treasured possession. It was not because you were more numerous than any other people that YHWH set his heart on you and chose you—for you were the fewest of all peoples. It was because YHWH loved you . . . You shall devour all the peoples that YHWH, your God, is giving over to you, showing them no pity. (Deut. 7:1–8, 16)

The third example that makes it clear that biblical texts cannot be the word of God literally revealed, in the fundamentalist sense, is one I will again choose from the New Testament. What Paul says in 2 Corinthians 3:4–4:6, in contention with his Jewish-Christian opponents, about the so-called Old Testament and especially the narrative in Exodus 34:29–35, cannot be evaluated as a revealed, authoritative interpretation of the Old Testament story, but rather as a pious deception[15] for a good purpose, although at the same time the history of its impact must be regarded as fatal:

> Since, then, we have such a hope, we act with great boldness, not like *Moses, who put a veil over his face* to keep the people of Israel from gazing at the end of the glory that was being set aside. But their minds were hardened. Indeed, to this very day, when they hear the reading of the old covenant, that same veil is still there, since only in Christ is it set aside. Indeed, to this very day whenever Moses is read, a veil lies over their minds; but when one turns to the Lord, *the veil is removed.* (2 Cor. 3:12–16, NRSV, italics added)

What must be considered in shaping a responsible theological treatment of these three texts, in order to leave behind any fundamentalistic biblicism and yet make it possible to hear these texts (and the Bible as a whole) as God's revelation? To me, the following five aspects seem important and indispensable:

1. The dignity of biblical texts as revelation cannot be rescued by applying the model (still very often used) of *evolutionary* revelation, according to which the texts of the so-called Old Testament that are felt to be problematic are said to reflect a still imperfect stage of revelation that is overcome in the New Testament. The two examples quoted above from the New Testament demonstrate that this is contrary to the evidence of the text itself. Would anyone want to say that the Song of Songs in the Old Testament and a proper interpretation of Genesis 2:4b-25 do not represent a view of sexuality and marriage that are far more acceptable for us theologically than 1 Corinthians 7:1–7? No, that individual biblical texts stand at a very different distance or proximity to what we today hear as the fundamental biblical message is true for *both parts* of our Christian Bible in equal measure.

2. Before we can begin a discussion of the claims of the text as revelation, we must make an effort, with the aid of historical criticism, *to understand* what the texts intended to say to their hearers or readers at the time of their origins. They were not formulated as timeless truths, but in very specific social and religious-historical contexts. Only when the original and current *contexts* form part of the reflection can the *texts* themselves be understood. This is true of *all* biblical texts, even those that appear to us to be less unwieldy.[16]

3. Biblical texts are always only partial elements in the *whole* Bible, the whole canon. There is no problem in setting the three examples quoted alongside other biblical texts that say the contrary, or at least restrict them severely. From that point of view also, individual texts cannot be absolutized; they are always in dialogue with other texts on the same theme. Methodologically, this means that biblical texts must be heard canonically. Texts on the same theme interpret one another. As partial texts, they have only a limited power of expression; they receive their deeper sense (*sensus plenior*), which goes beyond the meaning intended by the individual author, from the Bible as a whole.

4. The meaning of an individual text is also clarified from the context of the community of life and faith in and for which the text acquired its canonical validity. The same text can, therefore, have a different *reve-*

latory validity in Judaism and in Christianity. But it can also convey a differently accented truth at different times and in different places. Therefore the history of the impact and reception of an individual text in the annals of Judaism and Christianity must also be taken into consideration when we reflect on its revelatory character. In a particular situation, constructive and liberating texts like Deuteronomy 7 and 2 Corinthians 3:4–4:6, taken as a whole, can have been received in such a destructive way that the very knowledge of this negative history of reception becomes a constitutive part of the revelatory dimension of these texts.

5. Strictly speaking, it is not the individual biblical texts that are God's revelation, in such a way that the Bible would be a collection of revelations and eternal truths descended from heaven. Only the *Bible as a whole* is the revelation of God; that is, the record and reflection of the event in which God confronts God's people Israel and the church, individual human beings, and the whole world with God's own reality in such a way that they begin to understand themselves and their own way toward entry into communion with God. That is revelation as it occurs in the Jewish and Christian Bible: "In what we receive from God we learn to understand ourselves; we learn to be true human beings."[17] The Bible, with its very different testimonies to God, takes us with it into the fascinating process of seeking for God, into which people are enticed by the God who calls and comforts them. Therefore to accept the Bible as the revelation of God means setting out on the search for God by entering into dialogue with individual biblical texts; this route is never barred to us. Jürgen Werbick has described the process in this way:

> The fascination of the way opened, prepared and given to us in God's self-revelation constitutes the certitude of faith. This is the assurance that God can be found by those who seek God; indeed, that God enters into the search with those who seek, that God seeks with and among them and tries to see how God's saving rule can be received by human beings and change them. Seeking God with God, making the attempt together with God, is something daring, because we do not yet have what we are seeking. But we seek, we continue to question, because we have already found; and what we have already found is the basis for the joyful, calm, challenging confidence that it is good to go on seeking, to seek farther. That is the fundamental law of love.[18]

Against the background of these five considerations, we can say that the psalms of vengeance participate in the revelatory dynamic of the Bible within different contexts, and exercising different functions. Against all attempts to minimize or conceal the terror of everyday violence, and against the inclination of theology to marginalize the suffering inflicted on human beings by violence and to spiritualize it by example in public liturgy, these psalms confront us with the reality of violence and, especially, with the problem of the perpetrators of this suffering and their condemnation by the judgment of God. In the process, they very often compel us to confess that *we ourselves* are violent, and belong among the *perpetrators* of the violence lamented in these psalms. *In that way,* these psalms are God's revelation, because in them, in a certain sense, God in person confronts us with the fact that there are situations of suffering in this world of ours in which such psalms are the last thing left to suffering human beings—as protest, accusation, and cry for help. It is obvious on the face of it that these psalms are contextually legitimate on the lips of the victims, but a blasphemy in the mouths of the executioners, except as an expression of willingness to submit oneself, with these psalms, to God's judgment.

Thus these psalms have a manifold revelatory dimension, for whose sake they may not be eliminated from the Bible:

1. They can protect the victims of violence from becoming speechless and apathetic in the face of the overwhelming power of their suffering, or from feeling themselves the sacrificial victims of an incomprehensible divine wrath. When they struggle with God against God for the sake of justice, they keep open the question of God, even when they seem to be answered by the power of reality, to the detriment of those who suffer.

2. They uncover the potential for violence as a reality of human community life, and they cry out for change and for help. In their provoking and shocking images, they hold fast to the provocation and outrage that such a world experienced as hostile and violent represents, both in light of talk about a good God and in view of the human longing for harmony and peaceful wholeness. It is not these psalms that are provocative and outrageous, but human beings and their world. Because of this, we need these psalms. In them, God is personally confronted with this outrage.

3. As parts of the biblical text, the psalms of vengeance stand alongside other texts of the Bible that struggle against violence and in reaction to it, that speak of nonviolence as the way to overcome violence, and even dream of an end to enmity in the coming of the realm of the God of justice and peace. These "anti-violence texts" are found not only in the New Testament, but in especially large numbers precisely in the Old Testament. These texts, too, must be read and lived contextually if they are to unfold their socially transforming power, and not least in confrontation with the biblical "violence texts."

It should by now be clear enough that the kind of differentiation out-lined here can overcome both this-or-that alternatives and all types of fundamentalism, whether critical or uncritical. If the Bible, as revelation of God, is to confront the variety and multiplicity of life with God, the complexity of the individual biblical texts within the whole of the biblical canon must remain vital and valid.

4

Practical Consequences

Revitalization of Lament in Liturgical Prayer

The psalms of enmity confront us with violence—everyday, structural violence as something constitutive of our entire reality. As we said in chapter 3 (see "The Psalms of Vengeance: A Revelation of God?") that is their function as divine revelation. At the same time, their function is to teach us to say "no," and beyond saying it, to be compelled to cooperate in diminishing violence and enmity, as the clinical psychologist Udo Rauchfleisch describes:

> When we approach the topic from this ordinary perspective, we suddenly discover—surely with a shock—that violence is by no means something that always and only concerns "other people." Unexpectedly, we are faced with the fact that *we ourselves,* each of us in his or her own way, are not only victims of violence, but also its perpetrators. . . . No matter how great our hope for a world without violence, the lack of realism in such an idea is still greater. We must presume that aggression, in both constructive and destructive forms, is part of the fundamental makeup of the human being, and that therefore we must always reckon with violence in ourselves and in our fellow humans. However, we are not completely helpless in our subjection to these forces; we have a great variety of opportunities for dealing with it in different ways, for recognizing destructive developments at an early stage, and thus for preventing the worst from happening. We are the better equipped for this the more alert we are to these phenomena, and ultimately that means the more conscious we are of the violence dormant within our-

selves. . . . Violence stands behind us and threatens us; it may already
have taken possession of our house and forced us to serve it. Nevertheless, we hold up before this world filled with destructiveness
the vision of a better future, and we may hope that we will thus be
able to keep alive in ourselves at least a spark of hope, instead of the
flames of violence.[1]

The biblical psalms of enmity do not engage violence in a distant and an-
alytic manner, but in the form of lament and accusation—and not merely
lament over the destructiveness of violence, or in accusatory confrontation
with the perpetrators of violence, but in the form of a passionate question-
ing about God, or more precisely, in accusation against God's own person
in light of the so-called problem of theodicy. The psalms of enmity not only
articulate the catastrophic brokenness of human existence and its entan-
glement in a world distorted by suffering, but hold out against the imposed
rejection of assent to existence by holding up that rejection before God, in
lament and accusation. In this perspective, the psalms of enmity are the
most concentrated form of prayer: They reach out to God when everything
seems to speak against God. Where *everything* speaks *against* God, those who
pray them attribute *everything to* God.*

In order to comprehend this capacity of the biblical psalms of enmity, we
must rediscover lament in our liturgical prayer culture. In 1987, Ottmar
Fuchs, in an impressive analysis of our current Christian praxis and theology of prayer, wrote under the heading "Lament. A forgotten form of
prayer" a confirmation of something that the Protestant systematic theologian Otto Bayer had asserted some years previously:

From the earliest period of the church, lament has been nearly ex-
tinguished in worship and repressed in the daily life of Christians.
Wherever it breaks forth in its elemental guise it is formless, and finally, theological reflection has completely neglected it. It is true
that, in fact, it did not disappear, because the psalms of Israel were
accepted as the primitive prayers of the church as well. But liturgy
and theology by no means did justice to its fundamental meaning.
Even today, it does not constitute a significant point of view in dog-
matics or ethics, and it is absent from the systematic conceptual language of the standard handbooks and lexicons.[2]

This addresses the point from which we must begin the task of changing
our liturgical praxis. It is true that we recite the psalms of lament in the
liturgy, but we do not take account of them as *lament and accusation directed
to God,* because there is no liturgical provision for this form of prayer, and
because an accusation of God, strictly understood, is not considered a le-

* *Translator's note:* The author's German makes a word-play on *sprechen gegen,* "to speak against,"
and *zusprechen,* "to award" or "to attribute."

gitimate form of Christian prayer. As Fuchs points out, in the study previously cited, the section of "personal prayers" in the German prayer- and hymnbook, *Gotteslob* (pp. 17–42), for example, does not contain any laments:

> Why and whence this reticence . . . to make lament a formal prayer
> and thus to designate it as an act of speaking and so to present it (in
> an official prayer book of the German church) as also a church-approved and spiritually appropriate relationship to God? It is true
> that the prayers themselves mention a personal situation of need
> and the corresponding reaction of those who pray, but they turn all
> too quickly to trusting petitions, even to the point of surrender and
> willingness to endure everything! As a group, these prayers have a
> depressing and calming effect, and do not permit the process of
> questioning and lament in its demanding and aggressive form; instead, they actually suppress that confrontation and cover it over because of their extreme fear of conflict. Such an outcome is neither
> just to the situation of those who suffer, nor does it take seriously
> the biblical genres of prayer![3]

Thus it is vital that we restore lament to its rightful place in the liturgy as a necessary and legitimate form of prayer. Otto Bayer suggests two particular places in the liturgy that are also urgently in need of revision in the Catholic celebration of the Eucharist, and that could acquire new vitality from a deliberate shaping as lament:

> The church is church when it takes a just account, from the outset,
> of its solidarity with all human beings; that solidarity is expressed
> not least in questioning and lamenting. The assembled community
> of Jesus Christ cannot achieve this solidarity any better than in its
> use of the questions and laments in the psalms of Israel. The full
> consequences of theological reflection and liturgical praxis must be
> drawn [in the use of these psalms], especially in connection with
> the "Kyrie"—the cry from the depths: "Lord, have mercy!"—and in
> the prayers of the people.[4]

The metamorphosis of a Christianity sensitive to suffering into a Christianity primarily attuned to sin, which we criticized above (see chapter 3, "A Dynamic World Image and a Realistic View of the World") in agreement with J. B. Metz, could be the impetus to a revision here, if the so-called general confession of sins at the beginning of the eucharistic celebration were to lament not only the problem of sin, but the distress and suffering of the despairing and the sick, the persecuted and the dying—perhaps even with the use of a biblical psalm of lament. In the same way, the so-called prayers of the people would acquire a greater theological depth if they were formulated much more consistently as a lament in light of the problem of theodicy. Only when we experience this lament also as prayer in which we hear and mourn the suffering *of others* will we learn to accept the biblical psalms of enmity as a passionate struggle for the truth of God. I can therefore only agree emphatically with Gottfried Bitter, pastoral theologian of Bonn:

> I desire for myself and our congregations a revival of the prayer of lament—against our obvious apathy and against a dreaded passivity on the part of God, in face of our disappointment with this God and our own powerless protest.[5]

Practicing and Dramatizing the Psalms as Contextual Poetry

That the psalms as a whole, and the psalms of enmity in particular, are *poetic prayers* (cf. chapter 3, "Poetic Prayers") has consequences for their liturgical treatment. Certainly, there is such a thing as a spontaneous, intuitive and meditative encounter between an individual at prayer and a psalm text. Such encounters will be different, depending on the particular situation and individual disposition. But when the psalms are recited as common prayer (for example, in the Liturgy of the Hours or at the eucharistic celebration), there is need for practice and adequate liturgical staging.

Practice begins with becoming sensitive to the psalms as poetry—that is, gaining a feeling for their imagery and form. The preconditions for this are a poetic translation and a printed text that, as with poetry in general, reflects the structure of the psalm, and thus its dynamic as prayer. Our *Einheitsübersetzung* (the German ecumenical translation) fulfills neither of these desired conditions.

The liturgical presentation, whether as recitation or song, must be well prepared and carried out in a very deliberate manner. The most common alternating (antiphonal) chant, which uses the same melody throughout a psalm for lament, petition, and confession of hope, is not well suited for this purpose. I consider it much more appropriate to have the psalm sung by a cantor, while the congregation sings or speaks a suitable psalm verse (or an antiphon) at significant points indicated by the formal structure of the individual psalm. The congregation's psalm verse or antiphon can then evoke the contextual situation in which the particular psalm will or can become the revelation of God (cf. chapter 3, "The Psalms of Vengeance: A Revelation of God?").

We have already considered (in chapter 2, "Psalm 139: Passionate Struggle against Structural Violence"; "Psalm 137: What Remains for the Powerless") that, from the perspective of understanding the psalms as poetry, it is impossible to omit individual verses of a psalm, thereby destroying the psalm itself as a "work of art," and we gave examples from the text itself, using Psalms 139 and 137. It is a pastoral reality that in a congregation only a limited selection of psalms can really take root, and it is perfectly obvious that the selection must be made with particular sensitivity. But that this selection must eliminate every kind of opposing or discordant note is neither pastorally sensible nor theologically legitimate. In my opinion, *not a single psalm* may be or need be excluded from the church's official Liturgy of the Hours.

I can easily imagine that one may lessen the semantic shock of some images, and that some formulations that are known, on the basis of the aesthetics of reception, to evoke false connotations may need to be corrected. This could be done in such a way that the liturgical text contains a freer translation, while the literal text is quoted and explained in a footnote. Let me illustrate this with two examples.

The semantically quite shocking verses in Psalm 137:7–9 read literally (cf. chapter 2, "Psalm 139: Passionate Struggle against Structural Violence"):

Remember, YHWH, the sons of Edom
  the day of Jerusalem!
They said, "Tear it down! Tear it down!
  Down to its foundations!"
O daughter Babylon, you devastator!
  Happy the one who pays you back
  what you have done to us!
Happy the one who grabs and smashes
  your children against the rock!

Against the background of the explanations given in chapter 2 (see "Psalm 137: What Remains for the Powerless") I would represent this problematic section of the psalm in the following words, which remain very close to the original text:

O daughter Babylon, you devastator!
Happy the one who brings you to judgment
  because of what you have done to us!
Happy the one who seizes you
  and puts an end to your rule forever!

The entire psalm could be recited or sung in three sections: verses 1–3, 4–6, 7–9. The contextual antiphon to be sung by the congregation could be verse 1.

Similarly, the semantic shock produced by Psalm 58:10 (cf. chapter 2, "Psalm 58: A Cry for Right and Justice") could be lessened if another metaphor, almost identical in meaning, is chosen:

The righteous will rejoice when they see vengeance,
  when they bathe their feet in the blood of the wicked.

This is an expression of the wish that "all who take the sword will perish by the sword" (cf. Matt. 26:52), a projection of the longing for justice to triumph over injustice. It is presented here as a personified confrontation between "the righteous" and "the wicked." As a liturgical translation, one might choose:

> The righteous will rejoice in the victory of justice,
>> when they see how the power of the wicked collapses.

Of course, a liturgical version of the psalms of enmity must not rob them of their power to irritate. It should, instead, make one aware of the shock and the barb that violence, and suffering caused by violence, signify in these psalms, in spite of or even because of theological talk about salvation. The liturgical presentation of these psalms can even contribute to a cultural control of destructive aggressions, but only by placing them in the hands of God.

Reciting the Psalms of Enmity as Canon

The psalms of enmity offer us neither a dogmatic doctrine of God nor a summary of biblical ethics. These are poetic prayers that hold up a mirror to the *perpetrators* of violence, and they are prayers that can help the *victims* of violence, by placing on their lips a cry for justice and for the God of vengeance, to hold fast to their human dignity and to endure *nonviolently*, in prayerful protest against a violence that is repugnant to God, despite their fear in the face of their enemies and the images of enmity. The transfer of vengeance to God that is indicated in the psalms implies renouncing one's own revenge. That is also the overall biblical context within which the psalms of enmity have been transmitted to us.

Therefore the psalms of enmity must also be recited in a conscious knowledge of this canonical context within which they stand; that is, they must be seen and evaluated within the literary context of the book of Psalms and of the entire Bible, as *one* voice among the chorus of complex speech about and to God. As individual psalms, they have their situational *kairos:* Those who refuse suffering people the right to lament deny them their own language and thus a fundamental act of their humanity. On the other hand, we must consider that the book of Psalms deliberately places the genres of lament, petition, praise, thanksgiving, doubt, meditation on wisdom, and others side by side in a colorful mixture, and combines them in a variety of ways. Those who wish to enter into the book of Psalms must also surrender themselves to this complex view of the human condition, and in this way, they will traverse the depths and heights of human life with God. A canonical recitation of the psalms can preserve the idea, so important to the theology of the church's Liturgy of the Hours, of representative and solidary prayer in concrete form.

In practice, an attention to the canonical sense of the scriptures can have two consequences:

1. In a liturgical presentation, the psalms of enmity could be deliberately integrated into the canonical textual context in which they now *de facto* appear. The difficult Psalm 137 would unfold its dynamic as prayer especially if it were prayed in sequence, between Psalm 136 and Psalm 138. The "great Hallel" of Psalm 136 proclaims the fundamental statement of biblical hope in God in a series of variations:

   O give thanks to YHWH, for he is good,
   for his steadfast love endures forever.
   O give thanks to the God of gods,
   for his steadfast love endures forever.

   In light of this ancient experience of Israel, the full bitterness of that other experience of suffering that is lamented in Psalm 137 is understandable, as an outcry to the good God: How shall Israel sing a song of the good God "in a foreign land" except as a cry of protest and longing for right and justice? In fact, must Israel not fall silent in the face of the silence of its own God?

   By the rivers of Babylon—
   there we sat down and wept . . .
   How could we sing YHWH's song
   in a foreign land?

   In Psalm 138, then, "David" opens Israel's mouth with a recollection of the "Shema Israel," which Moses proclaimed to them:

   Hear, O Israel!
   YHWH is our God,
   YHWH alone.
   You shall love YHWH your God
   with all your heart,
   and with all your soul,
   and with all your might.
   (Deut. 6:4–5)

   The beginning of Psalm 138 recalls this basic confession and at the same time hearkens back to Psalm 136:

   Of David:
   I give you thanks with my whole heart;
   before (all) the gods I sing you my psalm.
   I bow down toward your holy dwelling,
   and give thanks to your name
   for your steadfast love and your faithfulness.
   (Ps. 138:1–2)

2. Another form of canonical prayer of the psalms organizes the difficult psalms of enmity in contrast with thematically related psalms in such a way that the praying community is drawn into a prayer-dialogue. This can also be exemplified by reference to Psalm 137. The destructive wish, "O daughter Babylon, happy the one who puts an end to your rule" (Ps. 137:8–9: see above, "Practicing and Dramatizing the Psalms as Contextual Poetry"), can be set in contrast with the vision presented in Psalm 87, according to which "Zion" will become the center of life and peace even for the "canonical" enemies of Israel:

1a YHWH loves his foundation
1b   on the holy mountains;
2a YHWH loves the gates of Zion
2b   more than all the dwellings of Jacob.
3a Glorious things are spoken of you,
3b   O city of God. [*Selah*]
4a "I praise Egypt and Babylon
4b   for the sake of those who know me;
4c yes, even Philistia,
4d   Tyre and Ethiopia:
4e   This one and that one were born there.
5a But Zion I call mother.
5b   This one and that one were born in her."
5c   For the Most High himself will establish it.
6a YHWH records as he registers the peoples,
6b   "This one and that one were born in her." [*Selah*]
7a Singers and dancers alike say,
7b   "All my springs are in you."

When Psalms 137 and 87 are staged as a prayer-dialogue, the liberating and healing power of the prayer to the "god of vengeance" can have its effect. In these psalms, human violence and divine nonviolence collide in such a way that injustice and suffering are not rendered banal, but at the same time the last word is left to the "God of life."

Suggestions for a New Language of Prayer

In his final lecture at Münster (quoted in chapter 3, "A Dynamic World Image and a Realistic View of the World") Johannes Baptist Metz called, in light of the church crisis that is fundamentally a *God-crisis*, for a revitalization of the biblical language we have lost:

Elemental crises demand elemental reactions. My suggestion is not immune to misinterpretation. It will seem to some much too radical, to others much too modest. Where, in fact, does a theo-logy come from that, if it is not to be unfaithful to itself and others, will continually seek to be just that: speaking about God, speaking about God in these times, in the time of the *God-crisis?* Where will this speaking about God come from; what is its basis? Does it arise from the language of dried-up traditions? From the language of books, or even of *the* book of books? From the language of dogmas or other church institutions? From the imagery of our literary fiction? From the puzzling language of our dreams? Speaking about God always stems from speaking to God; theology comes from the language of prayer. That sounds pious and subjects me, in the eyes of those who choose not to understand me in other contexts as well, to the suspicion that I, the political theologian, have made another turnabout, this time to piety and pious submission.

But let us make no mistake: the language of prayer is not only more universal, but also more exciting and dramatic, much more rebellious and radical than the language of current theology. It is much more disturbing, much more unconsoled, much less harmonious than that. Have we ever realized what has accumulated in the language of prayer throughout thousands of years of religious history (and even in polytheistic religions one speaks of a *monotheism in prayer*): all the outcry and jubilation, lament and praise, doubt and sorrow and ultimate silence? Have we, perhaps, oriented ourselves far too well to the tamed prayer language of church and liturgy, and nourished ourselves on too many one-sided examples from the biblical tradition? What about Job's lament, "How long?" or Jacob's wrestling with the angel, the Son's desolate cry, and the last word of the New Testament, "Maranatha"? This language is much more adept at resistance, much less soft and accommodating, much less forgettable than the Platonic or idealistic language with which theology strives to make itself attractive to modern minds, and by means of which it resists bafflement in the face of all the catastrophes and experiences of nonidentity.[6]

Because the human being does not appear in many official church prayers, God does not appear either—no matter how emphatically God is invoked. We have not yet comprehended that our traditional liturgical language has lost its innocence in Auschwitz. Could the barb of the psalms of enmity awaken us from our false Christian belief that everything can *really* be again as it was before?

Notes

Chapter 1. A Complex Problem

1. Quoted in Kurt Marti, *Die Psalmen 42–72: Annäherungen* (Stuttgart, 1992), 5.
2. Norbert Lohfink, "Was wird anders bei kanonischer Schriftauslegung? Beobachtungen am Beispiel von Ps. 6," *JBTh* 3 (1988): 36, with reference to T. Collins, "Decoding the Psalms: A Structural Approach to the Psalter," *JSOT* 37 (1987): 41–60.
3. Cf. Othmar Keel, *Feinde und Gottesleugner. Studien zum Image der Widersacher in den Individualpsalmen*, SBM 7 (Stuttgart: Verlag Katholisches Bibelwerk, 1969), 93–131. There is a good overview of the recent discussion on the theme of "the enemy in the psalms" in H. Schulz, "Zur Fluchsymbolik in der altisraelitischen Gebetsbeschwörung," *Symbolon*, n. s. 8 (1986): 35–59, especially 39–43.
4. For attempts to take the sting out of Psalm 149, cf., among others, N. Füglister, "Ein garstig Lied—Ps. 149," in *Festschrift für Heinrich Groß* (Stuttgart, 2nd ed., 1987), 81–105; E. Zenger, *Mit meinem Gott überspringe ich Mauern. Einführung in das Psalmenbuch*, 4th ed. (Freiburg, 1993), 53–60; G. Vanoni, "Zur Bedeutung der althebräischen Konjunktion w=. Am Beispiel von Ps. 149,6," in *Texte, Methode und Grammatik: Wolfgang Richter zum 65. Geburtstag*, ed. Walter Groß, Hubert Irsigler, and Theodor Seidl (St. Ottilien; EOS Verlag, 1991), 561–76.
5. From the introduction to the *Kleines Stundenbuch* (Einsiedeln and Freiburg, n. d.), 7.
6. Alfred Mertens, "Heute christlich Psalmen beten. Zugänge zum Psal-

mengebet auf dem Hintergrund moderner Psalmenexegese," in *Liturgie und Dichtung. Ein interdisziplinäres Kompendium,* ed. H. Becker and R. Kaczynski, Vol. 2 (St. Ottilien: EOS Verlag, 1983), 503.

7. *Kritischer Hand-Commentar zum Alten Testament* (Freiburg, 1899).

8. *Die Psalmen,* ATD 14–15, 10th ed., 1973 (Göttingen: Vandenhoeck & Ruprecht, 1950). English translation by Herbert Hartwell, *The Psalms: A Commentary* (Philadelphia: Westminster, 1962). Quotations are adapted from the published English translation.

9. Otto Knoch, "Altbundlicher Psalter. Wie kann, darf und soll ein Christ ihn beten?" *Erneuerung in Kirche und Gesellschaft* 4 (1989): 45–47.

10. Cf. the Latin text of this intervention in Vitus Huonder, *Die Psalmen in der Liturgia Horarum* (Fribourg: Editions Universitaires, 1991), 7 n. 11.

11. Heinrich Junker, "Das theologische Problem der Fluchpsalmen," *Pastor Bonus* 51 (1940): 74.

12. Emanuel Hirsch, *Das Alte Testament und die Predigt des Evangeliums* (Tübingen: Katzman, 1936), 26.

13. Ibid., 6–7.

14. Emanuel Hirsch, "Etwas von der christlichen Stellung zum Alten Testament," *Glaube und Volk* 1 (1932): 23.

15. Friedrich Baumgärtel, "Das Alte Testament," in *Die Nation vor Gott: zur Botschaft der Kirche im Dritten Reich,* ed. W. Künneth and H. Schreiner, 5th rev. ed. (Berlin: Wichern-Verlag, 1937), 106–7.

16. F. Baumgärtel, "Zur Frage der theologischen Deutung der messianischen Psalmen," in *Das Ferne und nahe Wort. Festschrift Leonhard Rost zur Vollendung seines 70. Lebensjahres am 30. November 1966 gewidmet,* ed. Fritz Maass, BZAW 105 (Berlin: A. Topelmann, 1967), 23.

17. Ibid., 24–25.

18. G. Hinricher, "Die Fluch- und Vergeltungspsalmen im Stundengebet," *BiKi* 35 (1980): 55.

19. Ibid., 56.

20. F. Buggle, *Denn sie wissen nicht, was sie glauben. Oder warum man redlicherweise nicht mehr Christ sein kann. Eine Streitschrift* [*For they know not what they believe. Or: why no one can be honest and remain a Christian. A polemic*] (Reinbek, 1992), 79–80.

21. Ibid., 86–87.

22. Ibid., 78.

Chapter 2. A Look at the Psalms Themselves

1. On this, cf. Wolfgang Huber, *Die tägliche Gewalt. Gegen den Ausverkauf der Menschenwürde* (Freiburg: Herder, 1993), 168–70.

2. Dorothee Sölle, *Die Hinreise. Zur religiösen Erfahrung. Texte und Über-*

legungen (Stuttgart, 1975), 155–64. Trans. David L. Scheidt, *Death by Bread Alone: Texts and Reflections on Religious Experience* (Philadelphia: Fortress, 1978), 119–26. The English translation includes the complete text of the psalm.

3.   Hans Schmidt, *Die Psalmen,* HAT 1.15 (Tübingen, 1934), 245.

4.   Hermann Gunkel, *Die Psalmen,* GHKAT 2.2, 4th ed. (Göttingen, 1926), 586, 589.

5.   Franz X. Wutz, *Die Psalmen* (Munich, 1925), 351.

6.   The following reflections take up some important observations made by Walter Groß in "Von YHWH belagert," in *Festschrift für Gunter Stachel* (Mainz, 1987), 149–59. These reflections add precision to my brief exposition of Psalm 139 in Erich Zenger, *Ich will die Morgenröte wecken. Psalmenauslegungen* (Freiburg, 1991), 242–53.

7.   Othmar Keel, *Schöne, schwierige Welt—Leben mit Klagen und Loben. Ausgewählte Psalmen mit Auslegungen* (Berlin, 1991), 69.

8.   Ibid., 70.

9.   Heinrich Groß and Heinz Reinelt, *Das Buch der Psalmen II,* Geistliche Schriftlesung 9, 2nd ed. (Düsseldorf, 1984), 86.

10. Alfons Deissler, *Die Psalmen. II. Teil (Ps. 42–89)* (Düsseldorf: Patmos, 1964), 157–58.

11. Cf. Annibale Bugnini, *Die Liturgiereform,* 426 n. 10. English translation by Matthew J. O'Connell, *The Reform of the Liturgy, 1948–1975* (Collegeville, Minn.: Liturgical Press, 1990), 498 n. 10.

12. *The Interpreter's Bible* (Nashville: Abingdon Press, 1955), 4:450–51.

13. On this, cf. Hans-Peter Müller, "Entmythologisierung und Altes Testament," *NZSTh* 35 (1993): 2 n. 5: "In the concrete, immanent aspect of the action of a transcendent YHWH one may see a positive advantage of the Old Testament over the New, something in which the former is not superseded by the latter, even for Christians."

14. Harald Weinrich, "Semantik der kühnen Metapher," in *Theorie der Metapher,* ed. A. Haverkamp (Darmstadt, 1983), 316–39, speaks of the "contradictoriness" of the metaphors that give them their "bold character."

15. Jürgen Werbick, *Bilder sind Wege. Eine Gotteslehre* (Munich, 1992), 70–71.

16. The close relationship of Psalm 83 to Psalm 46 is evident especially in the semantic tension in both psalms between the "uproar of the nations" (Ps. 46:4, 7; Ps. 83:3) and the "knowledge of YHWH" (Ps. 46:11; Ps. 83:19); Ps. 46:11 is a challenge to the nations, while Ps. 83:19 is a plea to YHWH.

17. In Pss. 2:2 and 83:4 ("take counsel together; plot"); 2:5; 83:16, 18 ("terrify"); 2:12; 83:18 ("vanish, perish"); 2:12; 83:15 ("set ablaze, kindle").

The structural parallel between the two psalms is important: "attack of the nations" against YHWH, with quotation of the conspiratorial speech; intervention of YHWH by "divine terror," in order to bring the nations to recognize the universal rule of YHWH.

18. Alfons Deissler, *Die Psalmen. III. Teil (Ps. 90–150)* (Düsseldorf: Patmos, 1965), 185–86.

19. B. Hartberger, *"An den Wassern von Babylon. . . ." Psalm 137 auf dem Hintergrund von Jeremia 51, der biblischen Edom-Traditionen und babylonischer Originalquellen.* BBB 63 (Frankfurt am Main: P. Hanstein, 1986), 222.

20. Cf. Walter Dürig, "Die Verwendung des sogenannten Fluchpsalms 108 (109) im Volksglauben und in der Liturgie," *MThZ* 27 (1976): 71–84.

21. Quoted from W. Dürig, "Die Verwendung," 77.

22. Latin text in W. Dürig, 76 n. 17.

23. W. Stärk, *Lyrik (Psalme, Hoheslied und Verwandtes)* (Göttingen, 1911), 196.

24. Alfons Deissler, *Die Psalmen. III,* 89–90.

Chapter 3. Toward a Hermeneutic of the Psalms of Enmity and Vengeance

1. Joseph Ratzinger, *Einführung in das Christentum* (Munich, 1968), 271. Translation of this passage is by L. Maloney. For a published English translation, see *Introduction to Christianity,* translated by J. R. Foster (New York: Herder & Herder, 1969).

2. "Unsere Hoffnung," I.4.

3. Gottfried Bachl, "Das Gericht," *Christ in der Gegenwart* 45 (1993): 397.

4. Ibid.

5. Jürgen Ebach, "Der Gott des Alten Testaments—ein Gott der Rache?" in idem, *Biblische Erinnerungen. Theologische Reden zur Zeit* (Bochum, 1993), 81–93, at 82–83. I am grateful to this essay for a great many suggestions. Cf. also Walter Dietrich, "Rache. Erwägungen zu einem alttestamentlichen Thema," *EvTh* 36 (1976): 450–72.

6. Jan Assmann, *Politische Theologie zwischen Ägypten und Israel* (Munich, 1992), 85–87, 93.

7. Johannes Baptist Metz, "Gotteskrise. Versuch zur 'geistigen Situation der Zeit,'" in idem, *Diagnosen zur Zeit* (Düsseldorf, 1994), 84–85.

8. Ingo Baldermann, *Einführung in die Bibel,* 3rd rev. ed. (Göttingen: Vandenhoeck & Ruprecht, 1988), 100–101.

9. Ibid., 91.

10. Martin Luther, *Von wahrer und falscher Frömmigkeit. Auslegungen des 5. und 22. Psalms* (Stuttgart, 1977), 150.

11. Psalm 22 is "played out" from the end to the beginning: Psalm 22:19 is taken up in Mark 15:24; Psalm 22:9 is worked into Mark 15:30–31; Psalm 22:8 is used in Mark 15:29; Psalm 22:2 is quoted and translated in Mark 15:34. This movement excludes the possibility that the hopeful end of Psalm 22 can be heard as well; this is also prevented by Mark 15:37 ("Jesus cried out with a loud voice and died").

12. For an argument against this "neo-Marcionism," cf. Erich Zenger, *Am Fuß des Sinai: Gottesbilder des Ersten Testaments* (Düsseldorf: Patmos, 1993), 20–27.

13. The impossibility of uprooting this cliché about the better, "new" wine in this context is evident from the work of Vitus Huonder, *Die Psalmen* (which is otherwise very useful in many respects). The following conclusion is found there (p. 188).

The imprecatory texts are part of sacred scripture. They make up that storehouse of faith that we revere as the word of God. But how are we to understand them? Where shall we locate them within a salvation-historical view of the Bible? Is an inspired text simply timeless? Such questions arise in light of similar statements, especially those according to which Jesus indicated that the claims of scripture can be related to times and situations, and especially that they are relativized "in the fullness of time." We must frequently recall his saying that new wine belongs in new wineskins.

This much-quoted logion of Jesus (cf. Matt. 9:16–17) is intended, in the first place, to protect the valuable (!) old wineskins from the young wine that is still fermenting—as well as the new wine that would be spilled if the old wineskins split. Incidentally, Jesus also expressly says in Luke 5:38 that old wine is better than new.

14. On this, cf. the noteworthy expressions in the new document from the Papal Biblical Commission, *The Interpretation of the Bible in the Church* (Rome: Libreria Editrice Vaticana, 1993).

15. For the interpretation, cf. Hans-Josef Klauck, *2. Korintherbrief,* NEB. NT 8 (Würzburg, 1986), 39:

From a religious historical point of view, the veil on the face of Moses is derived from ancient oriental priestly masks. The priest who wears such a mask when emerging from the sanctuary slips into the role of the divinity and proclaims the oracle in its stead. This custom has already been polemically reversed in Exodus 34. Moses only covers his face after he has proclaimed the word of God, before he returns to the sanctuary. The OT does not speak of obscuring the glory. That is an exegetical conclusion drawn by Paul—if we should retain that translation at all; it can be understood only in the sense of a piously deceptive maneuver: Moses *veils* the fact that the glory endures only a short time. Paul intends to *unveil* it.

16. Even a key statement such as "God is love" (1 John 4:8, 16) is only "true" in context. It is well known that, in the history of Christianity, it has rather often been "untruthfully" applied.
17. Leo Baeck, *Das Wesen des Judentums,* 7th ed. (Wiesbaden, n. d.), 31.
18. Jürgen Werbick, "Der Streit um den 'Begriff' der Offenbarung und die fundamentalistische Versuchung der Theologie," in idem, ed., *Offenbarungsanspruch und fundamentalistische Versuchung,* QD 129 (Freiburg: Herder, 1991), 32–33.

Chapter 4. Practical Consequences

1. Udo Rauchfleisch, *Allgegenwart von Gewalt* (Göttingen, 1992), 8, 242–44.
2. Otto Bayer, "Erhörte Klage," *NZSTh* 25 (1983): 260.
3. Ottmar Fuchs, "Klage. Eine vergessene Gebetsform," in *Im Angesicht des Todes. Ein interdisziplinäres Kompendium,* ed. H. Becker, B. Einig, and P.-O. Ullrich, Vol. 2 (St. Ottilien: EOS Verlag, 1987), 2:944.
4. Bayer, "Erhörte Klage," 271.
5. Gottfried Bitter, "Wie kann ein ohnmächtiger Glaube wieder lebenskräftig werden?" *Lebendiges Zeugnis* 39 (1984): 60.
6. J. B. Metz, "Gotteskrise," 79–80.

Selected Bibliography

Althann, Robert. "The Psalms of Vengeance against their Ancient Near Eastern Background." *JNWSL* 18 (1992): 1–11.

Brueggemann, Walter. *Israel's Praise: Doxology against Idolatry and Ideology.* Minneapolis: Fortress Press, 1988.

———. *The Message of the Psalms.* Minneapolis: Augsburg Publishing House, 1984.

Day, J. *The Psalms.* Old Testament Guides. Sheffield: JSOT Press, 1990.

Holladay, William L. *The Psalms through Three Thousand Years.* Minneapolis: Fortress Press, 1993.

Keel, Othmar. *The Symbolism of the Biblical World: Ancient Near Eastern Iconography and the Book of Psalms.* New York: Crossroad, 1985.

Kraus, Hans-Joachim. *Psalms. 1–59.* Minneapolis: Augsburg Publishing House, 1987.

———. *Psalms 60–150.* Minneapolis: Augsburg Publishing House, 1989.

———. *The Theology of the Psalms.* Minneapolis: Augsburg Publishing House, 1986.

Laney, J. C. "A Fresh Look at the Imprecatory Psalms." *Bibliotheca Sacra* 138 (1981): 35–45.

Mays, James L. *Psalms.* Interpretation. Louisville, Ky.: Westminster John Knox Press, 1994.

———. *The Lord Reigns: A Theological Handbook to the Psalms.* Louisville, Ky.: Westminster John Knox Press, 1994.

McCann, J. Clinton, Jr. *A Theological Introduction to the Psalms.* Nashville: Abingdon Press, 1993.

Miller, Patrick D. *Interpreting the Psalms.* Philadelphia: Fortress Press, 1986.
————. *They Cried to the Lord: The Form and Theology of Biblical Prayer.* Min-
    neapolis: Fortress Press, 1994.
Murphy, Roland E. *The Psalms Are Yours.* Mahwah, N.J.: Paulist Press, 1993.
Petersen, David L., and Kent Harold Richards. *Interpreting Hebrew Poetry.*
    Minneapolis: Fortress Press, 1992.
Seybold, Klaus. *Introducing the Psalms.* Edinburgh: T. & T. Clark, 1990.
Vervenne, Marc. "'Satanic Verses'? War and Violence in the Bible." In
    Swords into Plowshares: Theological Reflections on Peace, edited by Roger
    Burggraeve and Marc Vervenne, 65–126. Louvain: Peeters, 1991.
Weiser, Artur. *The Psalms: A Commentary.* Old Testament Library. Philadel-
    phia: Westminster Press, 1962.
Westermann, Claus. *Praise and Lament in the Psalms.* Atlanta: John Knox
    Press, 1981.